TRAINING THE DRESSAGE HORSE

Novice to Medium Level

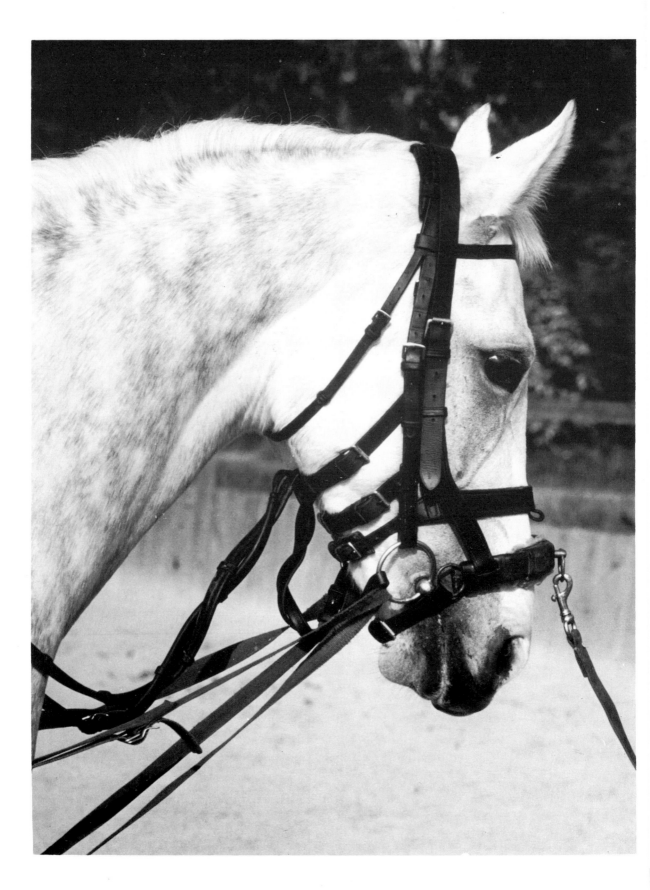

TRAINING THE DRESSAGE HORSE

Novice to Medium Level

Tricia Gardiner

Photography by Bob Langrish

WARD LOCK

A WARD LOCK BOOK

First published
by Ward Lock
A Cassell Imprint
Wellington House
125 Strand
LONDON
WC2R 0BB

Reprinted 1995
Copyright © Ward Lock 1994

Distributed in the United States
by Sterling Publishing Co., Inc.
387 Park Avenue South, New York, NY 10016-8810

Distributed in Australia
by Capricorn Link (Australia) Pty Ltd
P.O. Box 665, Lane Cove, NSW 2066

A British Library Cataloguing in Publication Data block
for this book may be obtained from the British Library

ISBN 0-7063-7146-1

Printed and bound in Great Britain by
Hillman Printers (Frome) Ltd

Frontispiece: A horse tacked up, ready for lungeing.

CONTENTS

Acknowledgements

I would like to thank Chris Spalding and Inch's Saddlery for equipment, all my clients who have so generously allowed themselves to be photographed, and Bill Noble who helped me put my thoughts on training into words.

6

CHAPTER 1

SELECTING THE RIGHT HORSE

This book has been written for the rider with some years' experience in one or other of the equestrian disciplines, and who has already developed a secure, independent seat and has a feel for, and an understanding of, the way a horse behaves and reacts under different circumstances.

It is intended for riders who are not only interested in competing in dressage competitions but who have enough knowledge to realize that the only way to learn more is to train a horse from the beginning, and who wish for the satisfaction that achievement of a goal after years of dedication and hard work can produce.

There are differing opinions as to whether it is better to buy a young horse and train it yourself, with the possible disadvantages of inadequate experience or knowledge in this sphere, or, alternatively, to purchase a 'schoolmaster' to learn from and compete on.

A really well-schooled horse will be very expensive to buy and, added to that, you still have to learn to ride it. Buying and old schoolmaster will at least enable you to feel different movements when you have learned to give the correct aids, for example, for shoulder-in, half-pass and flying changes. However, these horses are often in the twilight of their years or have been sold because they will not progress any further. They can be very stiff and unathletic, and, unless you are very lucky, they will not teach the aspiring dressage rider the correct 'feel' of working through the rein or how a horse should use his body. An old schoolmaster can be quite crafty in his assessment of a rider. If he is not as generous as he might be, he can often become difficult to ride and will need 'tuning up' regularly by an experienced trainer to keep him on the aids.

My advice is to get as much 'schoolmaster experience' as you can from reputable training centres and instructors, possibly even including trips abroad when possible, but, in the end, to buy the best young horse you can afford. Train it with someone who has proved that they are able to train horses successfully, who is able to ride the horse for you when necessary, and who can produce the correct feel for you during the different stages up the ladder to Grand Prix level.

If he is to succeed when competing at international level, the dressage horse of today has to be an athlete of Olympic stature. Much has been said about the training of such a horse and I do not profess to have found any new or unique method nor any short cuts along the way. The knowledge I have acquired comes from years of listening to successful and often famous trainers, from having had the good fortune to receive tuition from several very talented riders and trainers, from reading anything and everything on the subject of dressage, from competing at all levels, from observing the top international test riders over the last 25 years and, above all, from personally training as many horses as possible to Advanced level.

A well-proportioned horse with many excellent points and no serious faults.

The long-established principles of horsemanship have changed very little, although 'fashions' have come and gone and some changes of values have become evident, especially within the judging world. For instance, today most dressage horses are lighter, more elegant and have more Thoroughbred in their breeding than would have been seen 15 years ago when a heavier and extremely powerful horse, often of massive stature, was the norm. Also, a decade or so ago, judges liked to see a considerable bend in the neck during the half-pass movement. Whereas today more bend round the rider's inside leg is required but the neck is not so constrained, allowing the shoulder more freedom to take a big flowing step across. In earlier times, very few horses could perform an adequate piaffe, but with better training methods and possibly the inclusion of an obligatory 1 m forward in the piaffe steps of the FEI Intermédiaire II test, which was used for several years, the piaffe as a dressage movement has blossomed out of all recognition and it is now abnormal for a competitor in Grand Prix not to be able to show it. The inclusion of dressage to music in international competition has added considerable spectator appeal and, certainly, some freestyle music programmes can be very exciting and impressive. However, it is important that this form of entertainment does not override the classical ideals.

The classically trained dressage horse has a unique mutual understanding with, and confidence in, his rider. This is a further reason for buying and training your own horse. It is possible to miss out on this relationship if you only ride schoolmaster horses, who can seem like machines that operate if the right button is pressed, but do not perform the movements with any quality or expression. They have become used to so many different riders experimenting on them, that they are inclined to 'switch off' so that their work becomes dull. The object of the training is to develop, to as high a degree as possible within each individual's ability, the walk, trot and canter so that the rider is carried without tension or constraint and the horse willingly submits to their control and carries out the various movements requested with ease and generosity.

Choosing a horse

There have been many different types of successful dressage horses. Every rider has a personal ideal when considering the sort of animal they want to work with and it is obviously

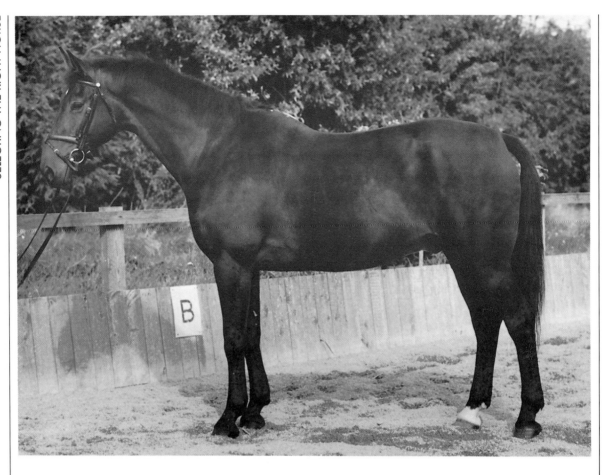

This horse has good conformation for dressage. The head is well set on to the neck, which arches up nicely from the shoulder. The front and the hind legs are of equal length – note that the line from the elbow to the stifle is approximately horizontal. The whole picture suggests symmetry although the hind legs could be considered a little too straight.

essential that the rider has empathy with the horse that they propose to start training. Of course, this does not apply to the professional trainer, who should be prepared, and able, to improve any type of horse.

Whatever type of horse or pony is chosen, certain characteristics and qualities will be similar to all of them to a greater or lesser degree, depending on how far up the scale they are required to go. A prospective Grand Prix horse must have as few flaws as possible, whereas a pony or schoolmaster need not be so perfect.

The most important requirement is a good temperament and with that I link trainability. It is not enough for a horse to be amenable in the stable and quiet out on a hack, he must also possess a very generous nature and must not become flustered or anxious when asked numerous questions in the school, some of which are not immediately understood. Nor should the horse mind being put under pressure occasionally. This side of the character is paramount, and the sensitive

Thoroughbred can have difficulty in coping with the demands of the dressage rider, especially if it is not always physically easy for him to comply.

The second vital requirement is three good athletic paces; by this I do not only mean producing technically correct steps, but also the agility with which he uses his body and the natural balance and power that has been bestowed on him before training has even started.

The overall impression of a natural equine athlete is of an animal moving in a light and agile way, most noticeable when the feet come to the ground - they do not make much noise because the steps are springy, and all the joints are working well, giving the impression of perpetual motion.

It can be an advantage to have a rounder action of the front legs than that required for a show horse, as this ensures a more classical piaffe and passage, where the foreleg has to be lifted higher than the hind leg. This is a difficulty that tends to

A very suitable type of child's pony, although because it has such well developed muscle under the neck and a naturally coarse head setting, a child would find it difficult to work this animal in a round outline. With correct training, however, the topline could be strengthened and the pony would be considerably improved.

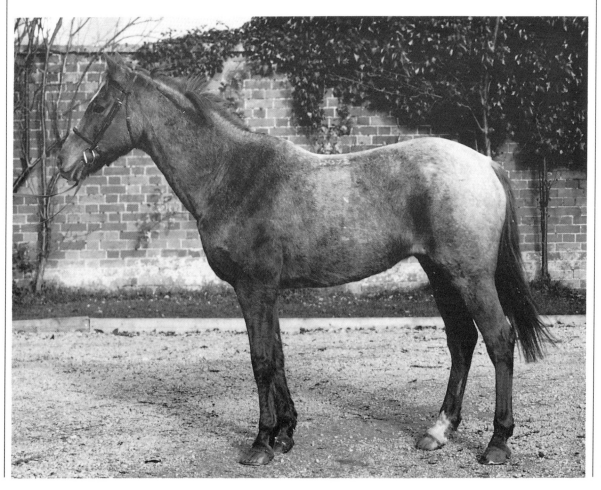

affect the Thoroughbred horse who does not naturally lift his knees very high.

The hind legs must be considered very carefully as it is essential that they are carried well forward under the body with every step, bending at the hock as they move to make a rounder step, not swinging under the body with a straight leg. The horse must appear to grow tall as he moves forward – no flattening or crouching should be apparent.

When the horse is being led in hand, look for a natural spring to the steps with an obvious use of all the joints. The hocks need to be strong and placed well under the horse, with no tendency for the hind feet to drag along the surface of the arena in walk and trot. When looking at the canter on the lunge, note how much the inside leg comes under the horse and whether the outside hind leg is used in a similar way, showing and ability to flex the hocks in this gait.

When assessing his potential, it is a good idea to watch a horse loose in an indoor school or paddock with good going, as one can then see his natural way of using the muscles in the neck, where the hind legs are placed without a rider and whether he makes fluent transitions and flying changes or only changes in front. Now is also a good time to listen to the noise of the footfalls. Some horses will make quite a thud as they move, while the springy horse is barely audible. However, beware of the possibility that the horse is merely highly excited, with head and tail up in the air, and covering the ground with impressive springy steps that might never be seen again under saddle.

Conformation

Lastly, consider the conformation. Athletes come in all shapes and sizes but, whatever his breed or type, the dressage horse must have the physical construction and musculature to be able to perform the work with as little hindrance as possible due to conformational defects.

For example, a horse that is croup-high is not going to be able to lower his hindquarter and 'sit' in the more advanced movements. Also, if his shoulder is lower than his quarters, he will never appear to be in balance and will often feel on his forehand and 'downhill'. If sway or dipped in the back, he will never look round enough in his topline. If the neck comes out of the shoulder rather low, he will be inclined to use the muscles at the bottom of the neck and not be properly rounded. There is also a problem if the shoulder is very long,

A very short-coupled horse that may have a problem in using his back correctly. The shoulder looks slightly heavy.

as required in the racehorse, because the horse will then have difficulty in transferring the weight of this big shoulder to the hindquarters, especially if the hindquarters are rather weak. This is often the case with Thoroughbreds. A long, sloping shoulder often goes with front legs that are much shorter than the hind legs. For dressage, it is better to have the stifles and elbows on one line parallel to the ground, as the joints in long hind legs have to bend far more to achieve the same result than if they were of equal length to the front legs. I have seen Thoroughbreds with 46 cm (18 in) difference in height from the ground between stifle and elbow and many others with no difference. The warmblood is more likely to have front and hind legs of equal length.

I like the head to show quality and intelligence, being not too long or heavy but with large ears and eyes that denote kindness and generosity. The setting of the head onto the neck is important as there must be plenty of room between the cheek bones and the top of the neck (known as the Vibourg's

13

A beautiful head and neck.

An awkward head to neck setting, leaving insufficient space between the cheek and the neck.

triangle) for flexion and the correct position required for collection. If there is not enough space in this area (the width of three fingers at least) it will be most uncomfortable for the horse to collect.. It is also worth ensuring that the lower jaw is large enough to accommodate the tongue comfortably, as a large, fat tongue, that is proud of the jaw, makes for bitting problems, especially when it comes to using a double bridle. A parrot mouth can also cause double bridle problems, as here the upper molars overshoot the lower ones, which leaves less space for two bits.

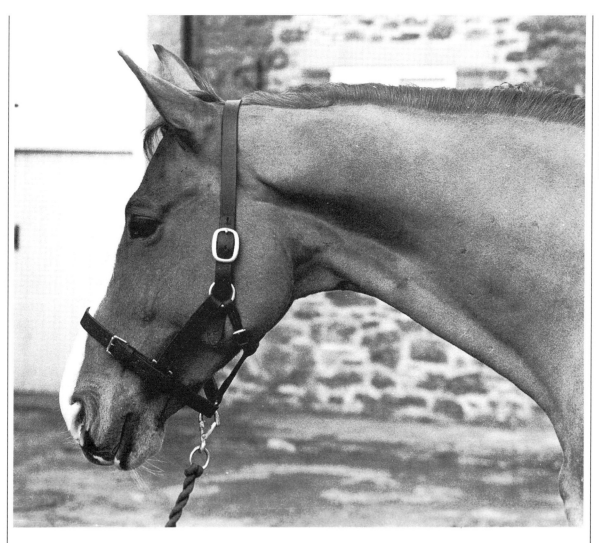

The head is well set on to the neck, showing plenty of room around the cheek bones.

The neck should not be too long nor too short and the depth of the neck at the base should not be too great – allowing plenty of room for the chest, which should be wide enough to allow the front legs to be set a reasonable distance apart.

The back must be strong and supple. Weak loins, that dip behind the saddle, are to be avoided. Equally, a roach back can also cause problems as it is easy for such a horse to resist against the rider with his strong back.

As with all competition horses, the limbs and feet must be as near perfect as possible, with no obvious flaws. When the steps are viewed from in front and behind, they must not be too close, otherwise the turns and circles involved in training will cause the hooves to knock the inside of the opposite joint, causing premature wear and tear.

15

A quality, Thoroughbred type of horse that is rather long in the body and would probably find galloping easier than engaging the hindquarters for dressage.

Many European countries have specialized in breeding warmblood horses with the temperament and physique suitable for dressage. The good-looking Thoroughbred horse usually has more quality but can lack rhythmic paces and a balanced conformation, as he has been bred to gallop with long hind legs and shoulders. Most of the time, of course, we have to put up with some features that we do not like. Some faults will improve with training as the horse muscles-up, for example, a weak neck. A small degree of dishing with both front legs may virtually disappear as the young horse develops and becomes stronger.

In my opinion, the ideal horse is a warmblood with as much Thoroughbred in his make up as possible without losing the workable temperament or acceptable conformation. Other breeds can be crossed with the Thoroughbred, for example, the Welsh Cob, the Irish Draught and the Cleveland Bay, but it could be said that to breed a top dressage horse this way would be the exception rather than the rule.

Having outlined the requirements for the perfect dressage horse, which, for most people, is impossible to find, it must be said that, given good movement and a workable temperament, the finished product is still approximately 75 per cent the rider and 25 per cent the horse. Let us now consider the best way to train the animal we have purchased so that the end result is a happy, uncomplicated, trusting and successful partnership.

A warmblood horse that is rather long in the body and with a forehand that is heavier than his quarters, making it difficult for the horse to remain in balance.

CHAPTER 2

EQUIPMENT AND TRAINING AIDS

There is a great selection of equipment for the dressage enthusiast to choose from and it is worth mentioning here some points to consider when buying new tack or updating various articles that are needed during training, especially when a new horse arrives in the yard. Attention to detail cannot be overemphasized, as damage or bad habits may be the result of making do with ill-fitting items. Over the years I have come across badly fitting bits, saddles and nosebands, as well as saddles that do not help the rider to sit in a correct position.

It is worth buying the best quality leather at all times. Avoid narrow straps that are likely to cut or chafe, such as those used round the chin on a drop or flash noseband. I believe 1.25 cm (½ in) to be the most comfortable and effective width in this case. Cavesson nosebands should be padded and, again, not too narrow. The padding should extend round the back of the jaw bones as well as over the front of the nose, to avoid any rubbing if the noseband has to be fastened tightly. It is preferable to resort to a well-padded, but tightly fitting, drop or flash noseband rather than a more severe bit, if the horse goes through a phase of being rather strong and disregarding the rein aids. This situation can often happen when the horse is asked to work with increased impulsion. However, the training must be such that the horse is not allowed to get strong in the rein when more advanced work is asked for; and to resort to a harsher bit then would be curing a symptom rather than sorting out a shortcoming in the training itself.

I also like some padding under the headpiece, as a drop noseband done up tightly will cause tremendous pressure over the poll and can aggravate the problem in a sensitive horse that is inclined to be fussy or tip his head. The tipping head is mostly caused by non-acceptance of the rein, together with an unallowing hand that is creating a stiff neck and back.

A correctly fitted snaffle bridle and flash noseband.

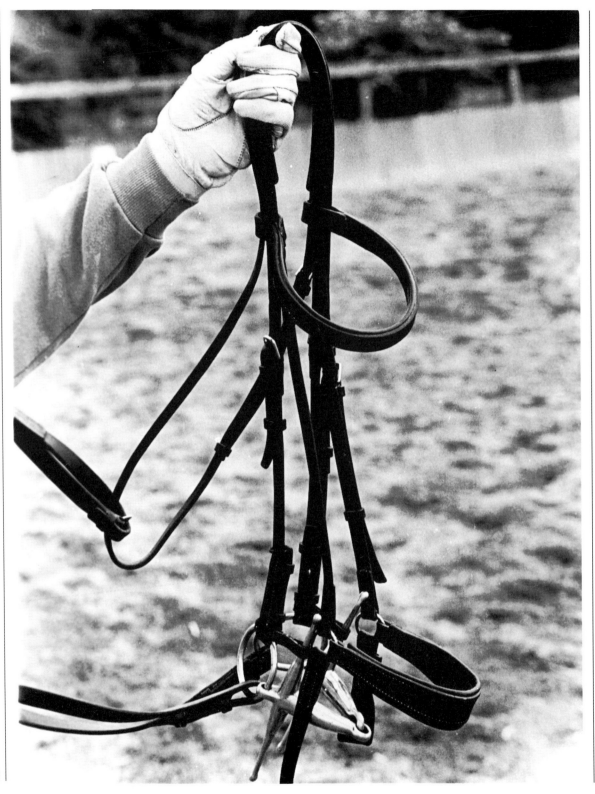

Above: **A different type of padding under the headpiece.**

Left: **A snaffle bridle with padding on the head piece and the front of the drop nose band. A thick strap fastens behind the lower jaw and has keepers to hold the cheeks of the Fulmer snaffle in place, thus positioning the bit across the mouth instead of letting it hang down.**

When the noseband is fastened tightly, sharp edges to the molars will press into the inside of the cheeks, while the bit knocking onto a wolf tooth may also produce an unstable head carriage. All of these possibilities must be looked for if the problem does not improve as the horse works more confidently into the rider's hand. Such confidence will not materialize if there is discomfort in the mouth or any other part of the head.

Bits

The width of the bit must fit the width of the mouth exactly. If it is too wide, an unnecessary nutcracker action occurs on the bars of the mouth, causing discomfort. Any discomfort from the bit will detract from the horse's inclination to accept the weight of the rider's hand and to this end, a thick bit, that covers a larger area of the mouth, is less harsh than, and thus

21

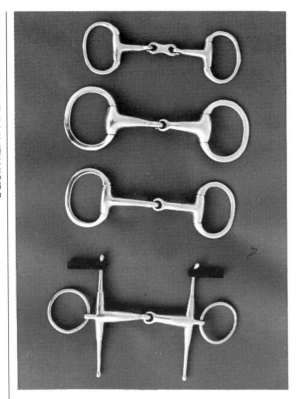

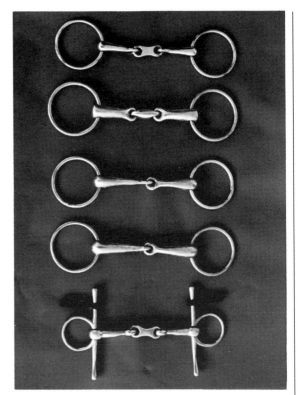

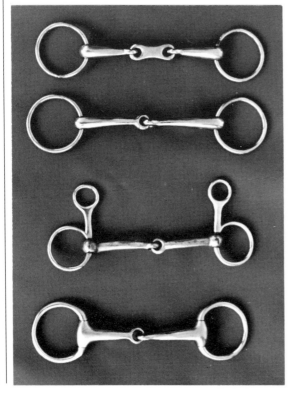

Above left from the top:
Eggbutt double-jointed snaffle
(French link); eggbutt snaffle
(thick mouthpiece); eggbutt snaffle
(thin mouthpiece); Fulmer snaffle
(leather keepers attatched).

Above right from the top:
Loose-ring, double-jointed snaffle
(French link); KK training bit
(thick mouthpiece); lightweight
German snaffle (mouthpiece
tapering to the joint); heavy
German snaffle; double-jointed
cheek snaffle.

Left: Bridoon and curb bits for a
double bridle. Both should be
made of metal. *From the top:*
French link, loose-ring bridoon;
loose-ring bridoon; fillis snaffle or
hanging-cheek bridoon; eggbutt
bridoon.

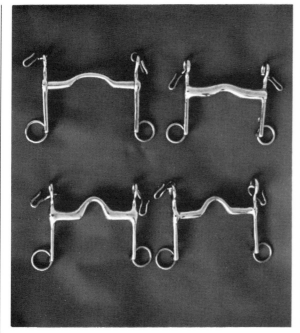

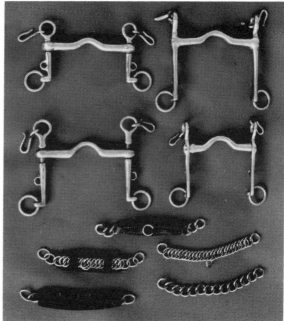

Top left: fixed-cheek Weymouth with a wide port; *top right:* fixed-mouth Weymouth with a small port; *bottom left:* Schulteis curb with a thick mouthpiece and high port; *bottom right:* curb with a thin mouthpiece and high port.

Left to right from the top: Tom thumb sliding mouthpiece with a small port; long-cheek, fixed-mouth curb with a medium port; sliding-cheek Weymouth with a port; fixed-cheek Weymouth with a medium port; leather curb chain; curb chain with a rubber guard; double-link curb chain; curb chain with a leather cover; single-link curb chain.

preferable to, a narrow one of the same design. A bit of 1.5 cm (⅗ in) is a suitable thickness at the ring end but it will allow more room for the tongue if this narrows towards the joint in the centre.

An eggbutt snaffle is the softest, mildest bit to use for a horse that is sensitive or shy in the mouth. However, if he is inclined to set his jaw, or leans on the rider's hand instead of carrying himself, a loose-ring snaffle is advisable. A double-jointed snaffle will often give more room for a thick tongue but, again, make sure that it is not of the thin and cutting variety as there is then a risk of the horse backing off the bit and not learning to work through the rein (see Chapter 3).

When it comes to selecting a curb bit, the mouth must be studied very carefully. One the whole, only a very large mouth

23

can cope with a snaffle and a thick curb bit and therefore a finer curb, with a port most suited to the shape of the tongue, must be found. It is advisable to try a variety of curbs to find out which is the most comfortable for your horse before rushing out and buying one, as this can be a very costly procedure. The shorter the cheek, the milder the action of the curb and I prefer to start with as least severe a bit as possible. (Refer to Chapter 8 for further information on the double bridle.)

Saddles

The shape of a dressage saddle is a personal matter. Nobody can select one for somebody else; they can only advise and point out the pros and cons. The saddle must be comfortable for the rider and fit the horse perfectly. Some people prefer a deep bucket seat, which supports the hips and pelvis in a correct, but rather inflexible, position, while others prefer a flatter seat where it is easier to move and adjust the weight and seat. There are also big differences in the design of the flaps, ranging from large blocks and knee rolls to keep the thigh well back, to virtually nothing except one saddle flap between the rider's leg and the horse's side. It is all a matter of personal preference and comfort. Riders who take up dressage after having spent several years in show jumping, eventing or hunting with their stirrups short and the knee bent, will often find a more forward-cut dressage flap to be the most suitable, until a deep seat has been established through riding without stirrups and stretching the correct muscles in the lower leg and thigh. When the thigh can leave the hip joint in a more vertical line, to bring the heel underneath the hip with as straight a leg as possible, the shape of the flap will probably have to be modified and a new saddle purchased.

Whichever design the rider chooses, it is essential that the bearing surface is flat and large and lies on the back muscles of the horse with an even contact, so that the rider's weight is uniformly distributed over as wide an area as possible, thus avoiding unnecessary pressure points. The depth of the padding must be such that the centre of the saddle is its lowest point. The rider cannot maintain a correct position if the front or the back of the saddle is too high and therefore a great deal of care has to be taken to fit a horse with a big shoulder and a back that dips away towards the loins, or, equally, a strong-backed horse with very little wither.

Girth straps can be long or short as preferred. The angle of a long back strap may be designed to hold the back of the

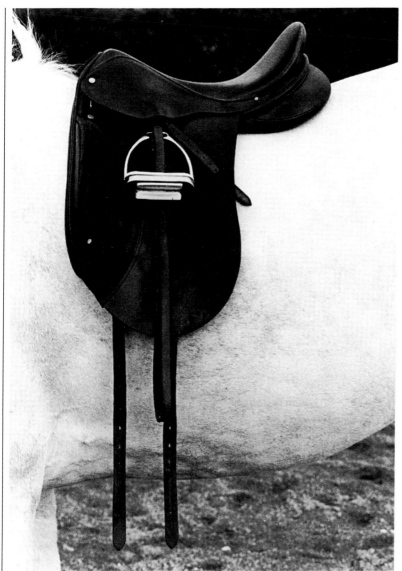

A well-fitting dressage saddle with panels designed to provide a large weight-bearing area in contact with the horse's back, thus reducing pressure on any particular section of muscle. Always try the saddle on first without a girth or numnah to assess the correct fit.

saddle in position and lessen any tendency to rock. The position of this strap should be flexible. If the horse has a round rib cage and a low shoulder, it would need to be set further forward than for a horse with a long back. Short girth straps make the girth easier to adjust but the buckles can interfere with the contact of the lower leg position. The girth should be soft to prevent galling, but strong and of a good width. Buckles should lie just above the elbows so that they do not produce any discomfort in this area.

Many saddles are made with a spongy substance under the leather of the seat, which can greatly add to the comfort of the

Left: Girth and numnah with the girth strap set at an angle to prevent the back of the saddle from rocking.

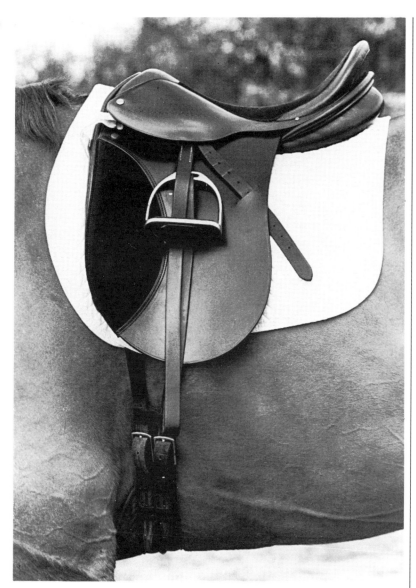

Right: A dressage saddle with suede knee rolls and seat, fitted over a square numnah.

rider with little padding around their seatbones. The whole saddle can be made in suede, or just the seat and knee rolls. There are many extremely helpful and knowledgeable saddlers who are only too willing to come and fit your horse correctly and to cater for any preferences you may have.

Numnahs

In theory, a well-fitting saddle, that has been custom-made for the horse, should need neither a numnah nor a pad. However, I believe that the muscles along the horse's back benefit from

27

A saddle with a synthetic, impact-absorbing gel pad used on top of a cotton numnah to reduce further the possibility of the rider's weight being concentrated over small areas, which can cause pressure sores. Note that the front of the pad must clear the horse's withers.

a gel pad or sponge numnah to relieve any tension or fatigue that can occur if the back becomes tired or the rider has a tendency to adopt a crooked position and not distribute their weight correctly. If the back becomes tired through too much sitting trot by the rider, the horse will tighten his muscles and learn to avoid using his body, to the detriment of his paces. This is to be avoided at all costs. If a favourite saddle that does not fit very well must be used on a horse, damage can be avoided through the use of sheepskin numnahs and pads, but for long-term use even this is not satisfactory and an individual saddle for each horse is advisable. If numnahs are not tied to the saddle correctly, they can pull down over the withers and cause a lot of harm. Equally, if it is not drawn up into the channel of the saddle to relieve this line of tension, a pad can pull the muscles away from each side of the spine. The fitter and harder the back muscles become, the better they will be able to cope with the saddle and the rider's weight. It is when the horse has had some time out of work that damage is likely to occur.

Lungeing equipment

The lungeing cavesson is a vital part of the training equipment and, like everything else, it must fit correctly. Lunge cavessons come in a variety of designs. I prefer the drop noseband type when breaking in and lungeing during training, as it gives more control if the horse is disobedient. However, it must fit comfortably under the bit. The width of the nose part can be too wide, making it impossible to fit well. If the young horse has a very small, delicate mouth or is ultra-sensitive to start with, it is better to use a cavesson-shaped noseband. Care must also be taken that this is fitted high enough not to pinch the skin between the bit and the noseband. The straps that fit behind the cheeks and jaw must be tight enough to prevent the outside cheek strap from being pulled into the eye while the horse is being lunged.

The lungeline should be about 10m (31 ft) long, light but strong and easy to hold. The lunge whip should be well balanced, comfortable for the user to carry and of sufficient length to touch the horse if necessary while working on a 15-m circle.

Side reins and running reins are also a necessary part of the lungeing equipment. Only side reins may be used when lungeing at affiliated dressage competitions. However, when training the horse at home, I prefer to use sliding running

The gel pad moulds itself to the horse's back.

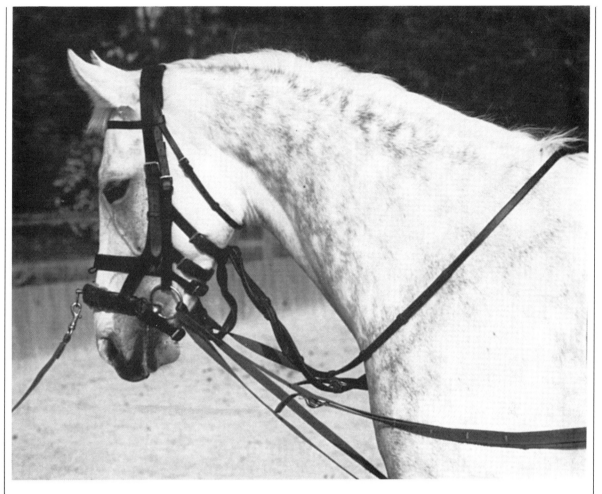

Above: **A Wells drop cavesson with one ring. The reins are twisted and held out of the way of the running reins by the throatlatch.**

Left: **A Wells drop cavesson with a cotton rope lunge line. This will give considerable control when leading a young horse that has not yet been introduced to a bridle.**

reins which enable the horse to move his head and neck more freely than a similar-length side rein. When the reins are fitted long enough for him to stretch his head and neck down low, he still cannot escape from the contact on the bit, as he could do in a side rein.

Some side reins have rubber circles inserted in them, supposedly to create a more elastic connection but, in fact, the movement they allow does not simulate the rider's hand and therefore they have little value. Side reins should be easy to fasten and adjust.

A lungeing roller is a necessity if breaking-in young horses. It should be provided with rings in various positions to accommodate side reins or for use when long reining. It is a useful piece of equipment when working older horses outside in bad weather, as it can be used in preference to spoiling an expensive saddle.

31

A horse ready to be lunged, with a nylon cavesson and side reins attached to a lungeing roller.

Boots and bandages

Boots are essential for protection when the horse is working on circles, to reduce damage if the horse knocks himself, which is especially likely when the horse is young and weak. They should fit well and snugly round the joint. If too loose, pieces of the arena surface can get in between the boot and leg, causing irritation to the skin and becoming a possible source of infection. Some people prefer to use bandages as there is then less likelihood of this occurring. However, only an experienced person should bandage a horse for work as damage can be done to the tendons if bandages are put on too tightly or the gamgee or Fibagee is not smooth underneath.

Bandaging is very time-consuming when compared with putting on boots with Velcro fastenings. Velcro should be kept clean to keep its holding power effective.

Whips, spurs, gloves and reins

During training, the schooling whip that the rider carries should be long enough to touch the horse behind the rider's leg without taking a hand off the rein. A light touch with the whip must be given if the horse disregards the leg aid or becomes sluggish in response to the aids. A young horse may be nervous of such a long whip initially and therefore a shorter one should be used at first. Whips may be carried at all UK national competitions except at any of the championships.They are not allowed in international competitions and therefore the rider must not train the horse in such a way that they cannot create maximum impulsion without the use of a whip. From the very beginning of training, the horse must learn to go forward from the leg.

Spurs may be used in all competitions and are obligatory from Medium level upwards. They can vary a great deal in severity and, in my opinion, should not be used in early training until the horse responds really correctly to the leg. A horse that becomes dead to the spur because spurs have been misused is not a pleasure to ride and will seldom train to Grand Prix showing the required elasticity and spring in his movements.

Gloves must be worn in competition and, as they help the rider to hold the reins in a relaxed manner, without tension in the fingers, they should be worn as a matter of course. When lungeing or leading a young horse, gloves will protect the hands from damage if the horse should become frightened or playful and pull away.

Most riders have a favourite type of rein. Bars or rubber will prevent the reins from slipping through the hand. These can also be used on the bridoon rein of the double bridle. A very narrow rein should be avoided as it causes tension when held securely and slips through the fingers if held lightly. The curb rein on a double bridal is narrower than the snaffle rein but should not need to be held so firmly.

Training aids

The most valuable equipment for a rider who does a lot of training alone is mirrors set round the arena. If possible, one

33

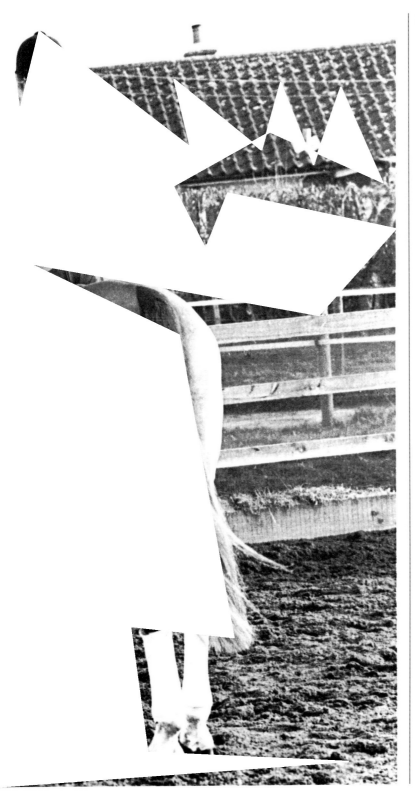

It is very useful to have a mirror at the end of the centre line in order to check the horse's straightness and your own position.

Always introduce a young horse to the mirror tactfully as some horses are frightened by their reflection. This one seems to be admiring himself!

should be placed at the end of the centre line, to evaluate the straightness, and another should be positioned at the end of a long side, to assess the angle and bend of the shoulder in travers, etc. In an indoor school the more mirrors you have the better, as there is much benefit to be gained from seeing the horse's outline, whether the nose is in front of the vertical, how far under the body the hind legs step and the length of the strides, etc. The benefit of 'seeing' what they are 'feeling' gives the rider a tremendous advantage over those working without mirrors.

Another very useful item is a video camera plus an extremely patient long-suffering and knowledgeable operator! The value of riding through a test the day before a competition and then assessing what the judge is going to see is a great help, as is watching the competition tests at a later date. The ability to keep a library of tapes, to see how the training is progressing or to refer back to a particular lesson or important occasion, is a benefit of modern technology that the competitive dressage rider should have access to if at all possible.

CHAPTER 3

LUNGEING THE HORSE AND RIDER

A horse ready to be lunged, with saddle, bridle, boots, cavesson, lunge rein and running reins fitted loosely.

If well grown and strong enough, the horse should be broken in at three years old, having already been well handled since he was a foal. The young horse must have plenty of freedom in his formative years but if he is allowed simply to roam in a wild state, without human contact, handling and breaking can be very traumatic and a great deal of time will need to be spent on gaining his confidence. The process will then take much longer than if he had been taught to tie up, lead in

hand, have his feet picked out and trimmed by the farrier, brushed over and generally handled and taught some manners right from the beginning.

Many difficulties can occur if breaking in is not done correctly. It is not a task for the inexperienced, nor for anybody working alone. Therefore, if you do not have knowledgeable help and sufficient time to do the breaking yourself, send an unbroken horse to a good professional and have him home when he is quiet to ride about. The benefits of this professional thinking and working along the same lines as yourself are obvious.

At the start of his early training, the horse must be confident and relaxed on the lunge before he learns to cope with a rider's weight. However well he has been broken in, it is still a stressful situation for the young horse to return home and be worked by somebody else. Two or three days' lungeing, before being ridden, will establish confidence in his new working surroundings.

Lungeing is the first step on the long ladder to developing the horse's physical and mental ability so that he will be able to perform the exercises required of him during his training to be a top-level competition horse.

In lungeing, the horse is worked on a circle in order that he will learn to accept control by the trainer through the lunge line, in conjunction with obedience to the voice and the whip. If done properly, this should produce a horse that is respectful, trusting and co-operative.

There are many other reasons for lungeing horses and the technique can be used throughout the whole training but it must be done skilfully and correctly, with the right objectives in mind. Initially, it is used for breaking-in and thereafter it is useful in further schooling through to advanced work in hand. It is also used for exercising and muscling-up horses that are not able to be ridden, for strengthening and retraining weak or problematic horses and for training riders.

Breaking-in

This subject is not being covered in any detail in this book as we are dealing with the training of a horse that has already been broken-in. However, a chapter on lungeing must emphasize what is expected of the horse during this phase of his career, as continuity and confidence are vital in the early stages and it may be necessary to go back to the breaking-in procedure after the young horse has had his first holiday or lay-off, depending on his character, youthfulness and attitude to being saddled and worked again.

In breaking-in, lungeing first establishes obedience to the voice, the whip and control through the line. The horse then becomes accustomed to a bit in his mouth, a lungeing roller, side reins and, lastly, a saddle. He must learn to walk, trot and canter on the lunge wearing all this equipment before doing the same thing with a light rider on his back. During this time he will begin to strengthen and develop the correct muscles and will become generally fitter.

If the reader has sent a young horse away to be broken-in and it has just returned, or has purchased a recently backed youngster, a sensible policy is to establish a good relationship on the lunge before any ridden work is attempted. In this way you will be safeguarded against any misunderstandings, due to nervousness or disrespect, that may occur when a new trainer is involved. The horse must become accustomed to a strange voice, possibly giving slightly different words of command, and a new location for the work. All these things can cause tension and mistrust, so plenty of time must be allowed to overcome them and familiarize the youngster with his new situation. He must submit willingly to the demands of working freely forward so that, gradually, his steps will become more positive and deliberate, which signifies that he is relaxing.

Muscling-up on the lunge

Lungeing is the most effective way to start muscling-up a young horse correctly or, equally, to improve a spoilt or badly muscled horse. For example, a horse that has been racing may have very adequate steps but will have developed muscles that are not desired in the dressage horse, such as those underneath the neck. On the lunge, such a horse can learn to work in a round outline. Eventually, the development in the muscles under the neck will disappear because they are no longer being used and the horse will be able to develop a topline and a stronger back before having to carry a rider and work in a different shape to that which he had when racing.

Lungeing overfresh and excited horses

Lungeing is an ideal way of coping with underworked horses that, for some reason or another, have spent too many hours in the stable without exercise. They can let off steam on the lunge without being a danger to anyone, but a very fresh horse can be a problem to control and so I advocate a lungeing cavesson that fastens under the bit in a drop-noseband design (see page 29).

I do not like to lunge directly from the bit as it ruins the horse's attitude to any reasonable contact on his mouth when being ridden and teaches him to be rough and crude in the mouth to any restraint from the rein aids. However, if it is a case of either controlling him or not, it is safer to run the lunge line through the inside bit ring, up over the head, behind the ears and then attach it to the outside bit ring. This is a very severe form of control, similar to riding a strong horse in a gag snaffle, and should be avoided if at all possible. Another form of control from the bit is to join the two rings behind the chin with a coupling strap which has a ring attached. With the lunge line attached to this ring you get an uneven pull, so this is not very good for the mouth but it is less severe than the former method.

Care must be taken when using side reins on an overfresh or excited horse as, if they are fastened when he is bucking and jumping about, he can give himself a nasty bang in the mouth, panic and throw himself over backwards. Side reins should only be fastened when the horse is moving in a calm manner.

Correct technique for daily work on the lunge

Lungeing must always be done on a soft, but not deep, surface, as no horse can develop a powerful springy rhythm if asked to circle on hard ground. One end of an indoor school or a fenced, all-weather surface is the ideal place to carry out the work.

At the stage of training that we are considering, the young horse is saddled and bridled and then the brushing and over-reach boots and the cavesson are put on. The side reins should be attached to the saddle only, not to the bit rings, and the reins of the bridle should be twisted and linked through the back strap of the cavesson.

Initially, the horse is allowed to go round on the side that is easier for him, i.e. not his stiff side, obeying the commands to halt, walk and trot. The whip is used to back up the voice if this is disregarded. The side reins are not connected during this loosening-up stage and the horse is encouraged to work on as large a circle as possible, with the trainer prepared to walk a circle, slightly behind the horse, so that they can

drive him forward. If the horse is high spirited, he is allowed to play and have a little buck but not to be seriously naughty and never to be disobedient.

When the horse has settled down and is relaxed, he must be brought back to halt, on the line of the circle, allow the trainer to walk up to him while remaining in halt, have the girth checked and the side reins or running reins attached. The side reins should be of equal length on both the inside and outside of the circle. A bend in the neck is not desirable as it can cause problems that cannot be dealt with when the trainer is on the ground.

The serious work now begins. The horse must first show a willingness to establish a position that stretches the whole of his topline, thus relaxing his back and neck and not rejecting a connection to his mouth at the end of a long side or running rein, with the nose being carried as low as the knees.

Once this outline and way of going are established they can

A horse working well on the lunge in a correct outline. He looks relaxed, active and happy.

41

Lungeing a young horse in a lungeing roller and side reins. The horse is working long and low, stretching his top line.

be used at the start and finish of work sessions throughout the horse's career, whether on the lunge or ridden, and can be resorted to at other times during training if tension and stress have overruled the ability to be supple and flexible and the movement through the back has been lost. The horse should be worked equally on both reins on the lunge: twice in each direction for about five minutes is usually sufficient if he is going to be ridden as well. However, some horses take longer than others to loosen up and work round and, as with all training sessions, it is better to finish having achieved a good result than to work to the clock.

Cantering

It often takes a long time for a horse to canter on the lunge in a relaxed, well-balanced way. The trot can be well established in a correct working outline, whereas in canter he is still floundering around and changing his legs, unable to find his balance. A small horse is less likely to have this problem than a large one. If this problem does arise, time must be given for the muscles and balance to develop so that cantering becomes easier, and the horse must not be made anxious nor forced to do something that he finds difficult on a small circle. As his physical condition improves, so will his balance, rhythm and co-ordination, resulting in enhanced paces. Until this happens, the trainer must walk vigorously on a circle so that the horse learns to canter on a larger circle, say, 25–30 m,(82–98 ft) making many transitions from canter to trot and back to canter again. With repetitive work and relaxation, the canter will improve and the horse will gradually manage a smaller circle. The canter must not be neglected just because the horse finds it difficult.

Observing your horse on the lunge regularly, especially if you work alone, enables you to assess the length of the steps and the use of the joints, the suppleness and the movement

No contact through the lunge line.

43

in the back producing a swing in the tail from side to side. The horse should be praised when working well. As a round outline develops and can be maintained during transitions and changes of gait, the side reins may be very gradually shortened but never to the extent that the nose is forced behind the vertical. The emphasis must be on movement from behind, created by the voice and the whip. When the horse can canter well and make canter to trot transitions easily, this will develop more impulsion in both gaits. He will learn to lengthen his stride in trot and, later on, will develop medium trot and canter on a large circle and more collected gaits on a smaller circle. The trainer must have complete control of the speed at this stage and the horse must not be allowed to run and lose the rhythm when attempting lengthened strides.

Having built the work up to create a shorter outline and more engagement (relative to the horse's age, physical condition and ability) it is then necessary to lengthen or unclip the side reins and let the horse stretch long and low again and then finish with a walk uninhibited by any connection with the mouth. Indeed, in the early stages the horse should only walk on the lunge with extremely long side reins for fear of spoiling the walk steps.

Moving about the forehand on the lunge

Another useful exercise during the lungeing session, which I find very helpful, is teaching the young horse to yield to the whip as in leg-yielding. When it is time to change the direction from a left- to a right-hand circle, bring him to a halt, walk up to him and stand by his shoulder facing the saddle. Hold the lunge line in your left hand, with a contact on the cavesson, and, with the handle end of the lunge whip, tap him just behind the girth just as you would nudge him with your left leg if you were riding him. The required result is that he should step away from the stick, carrying his hind quarters to the right. The hindquarters should turn about his forehand, which should stay more or less on the spot until he has completed a 180-degree turn. The horse should be rewarded after each step and should stand again in halt when he is facing the new direction so that you can walk round and start lungeing him to the right. On the whole, horses do not like stepping sideways, therefore it is a great help to teach him to cross over his hind legs in this way, before asking him to do the same with a weight on his back.

Pole work on the lunge

When a horse is really established on the lunge, a useful method of encouraging him to use his back and bend his joints is to introduce trotting poles into the circle. I place about five poles in the corner of the arena, leaving enough space for the horse to circle round the outside of them so that he can become thoroughly used to them lying on the ground. To start with, he must be led through the poles and walked up and down the line. As they are placed like a fan or rays of the sun, it is not difficult to find a suitable walking distance. Then, having trotted the horse round the poles for some time, a helper should pull one pole out towards the line of the circle. When the horse will trot over this quietly, another two poles can be added to make three. Do not put only two poles in the horse's path as he may decide to jump them and this will hurt his mouth if he is wearing side reins. Leave enough space between the poles so that this does not happen. After a short while, he should be able to trot over five poles placed on the inside of the track. On the smaller circle, the poles will be just under 1 m (3¼ ft) apart and on the outside, larger circle they will be 1.5 m (nearly 5 ft) apart. It is a test of utmost control to judge the length of your horse's stride and steer him on the right line down the poles. It is very noticeable how much more active the steps become over the poles and this activity is also maintained during the canter. Obviously, the cantering must be done well away from the trotting poles but it is important to include cantering during these exercises. If cantering is neglected, the trot will develop at a far greater rate and this will be a disadvantage when it is time to start competing.

The trotting poles will put a considerable strain on a young horse's muscles and should not be used excessively. Three times down the poles in each direction each day is sufficient for the first week or two and from then on the work should be increased very gradually.

Good lungeing is an art that takes years to perfect and it should be given just as much thought and effort as riding the horse. In ideal circumstances, the contact of the lunge rein on the nose of the cavesson is comparable to the connection the rider makes with the rein on the horse's mouth. The trainer should stand in line with the horse's hip, pivoting on their inside heel, if they want to work the horse on a perfect circle. However, a better relationship and more control can be established by walking round in a small circle a little behind

Trotting poles positioned for lungeing and also for use when riding on a circle or on a straight line down the long side of the arena.

the horse, from where it is easier to encourage him forward with the whip when necessary. Gloves should always be worn, to avoid injury if the lunge line is pulled through the hand quickly, and a hard hat is advisable when lungeing a young horse. The horse should never be lunged for too long and small circles should not be asked for until the horse is physically fit enough.

Lungeing the rider

While on the subject of lungeing, it is as well to mention the rider on the lunge. Although I am not dealing here with the novice rider, who, ideally, should spend a lot of time on the lunge, establishing their basic seat in the saddle, learning to balance and how to give the aids, there is still a definite advantage for the more experienced student to continue riding without stirrups and to have lunge lessons from a good instructor whenever possible. This will help them to keep a correct position, sitting on their seat bones in the deepest part of the saddle. When viewed from the side, there should be an imaginary vertical line running through the rider's ear, shoulder, hip and heel. To keep this position, and remain balanced while performing all the necessary exercises to train the horse, all riders should go to some lengths to keep fit and not let their muscle tone deteriorate.

Unless care is taken to maintain a classical position, it is easy to fall into bad habits such as sitting crooked, drawing up the knees and gripping too much, causing tension down the leg. In this situation the weight of the upper body comes off the seat bones and the heels draw up while giving the leg aids. Ideally, someone on the ground can point out these faults as they occur and, when on the lunge on a suitably quiet horse, it is possible to concentrate on them in a relaxed atmosphere.

The young horse should not be used for lunge lessons as his muscles and joints are not strong enough for prolonged sitting trot and he may not be quiet enough to allow the rider to relax and ride without holding the reins. It is the instructor's responsibility to control the horse during these lunge lessons and so it is an advantage to know the horse well, and if possible, use an old schoolmaster who is programmed to the work and answers well to the voice. A good lunge horse should not be abused by too much use and must be given other work to keep him interested.

The same equipment should be used as mentioned on page 29, along with a saddle that fits the rider and the horse. A

A rider sitting correctly in preparation for a lunge lesson. Note the straight line through the shoulder, hip and heel and also from the elbow through the wrist and on down the rein.

pad should be used to save the muscles along the horse's back from getting tired and the lesson should not last more than 30 minutes, which will include rest periods and the necessary discussion between rider and teacher. It is worth remembering that somebody in the centre of a circle cannot assess the rider's straightness very easily and so another person must check the rear view of the rider from the outside of the circle. However, it is better to correct the position from the side first and then from behind.

The correct basic seat can be achieved by simple exercises. First, sit in a relaxed and upright manner in halt and take the feet out of the stirrups. Then draw the knees up above the

47

horse's withers in flat-racing-jockey position. It should now be easy to feel the lowest part of the pelvis (the seat bones) against the saddle. The base of the seat should now be made as wide as possible before, very slowly, lowering the legs down to their normal length without lightening the weight of the upper body from the seat bones. Having thus established a deep seat, the rider can now hold the pommel of the saddle with both hands and lift the legs, at first one at a time in halt, away from the side of the horse in as straight a position as possible, i.e. without bending the knee, and then allow the leg to relax back against the horse's side with as deep a knee position as possible and the soft contact of the lower leg more secure than that of the knee, which should be very relaxed. When each leg has grown used to this treatment, both can be lifted away simultaneously in halt and then again at walk. A very athletic and supple rider can also achieve this exercise in trot and canter.

Maintaining a good position in trot.

The first exercise on the lunge is to allow the arm to hang down to get rid of any tension in the arm or shoulder.

For the more experienced rider, the lessons on position on the lunge are intended to correct the classical position and work on any tensions that may have crept into the neck, shoulders, upper arms, back, hips and legs. Being aware of stiffness and then being able to relax the necessary muscles in a controlled way is the key to keeping a supple, balanced position so that the aids may be given correctly and without constraint.

Exercises on the lunge

I am not a great believer in too many exercises for the rider on the lunge. It is the ability to practise keeping the position in a relaxed way that is paramount. However, any exercise

49

that helps an individual with their own particular problem is of value, as are exercises off the horse, especially breathing and toning the muscles as in keep fit classes. Swimming is one of the most satisfactory activities as it exercises the lungs, muscles and joints without any stress. Aquatrim classes can also be most beneficial.

Listed below are the most usual exercises that can be done on the lunge, each relating to an individual rider's require-ments and capabilities as advised by an experienced instructor. Exercises should not be carried out too arduously at first and must also be done in a relaxed rhythm. If tension or apprehension creeps in, they must be stopped.

It is as well to take some really deep breaths before start-ing on any exercises as, without sufficient air reaching right into the bottom of the lungs, the muscles will be deprived of oxygen and will not function or relax properly.

1   Most riders develop some stiffness at the back of the neck. This is caused by carrying the head too far forward instead

The rider is lifting the knees up to check and improve on equal weight on the seatbones.

Lifting the leg away from the saddle and then lowering it into the correct position.

of correctly balanced on top of the spine. Slowly lift the head up and back until it will go no further. Bring the head down until the chin is resting on the chest. Turn the head slowly to the right and then to the left as far as it will go. Repeat this exercise no more than four times.

2 To stretch the sides of the neck, roll the head to each side so that the ear moves towards the shoulder.

3 To loosen the shoulders, move the point of the shoulders in a backwards rotation, making a slow, rhythmical circle that rises up to the ear and then down as low as possible. Repeat six times forwards and six times backwards.

4 Arm exercises will also loosen the shoulders. Hold onto the front of the saddle with one hand and swing the other arm slowly in a backwards circle so that the arm is vertical as it passes the head. Some circles may be made with the elbow slightly bent before straightening it completely. Repeat with the other arm.

5 To loosen the waist and lower back, raise both arms to the side so that they are level with the shoulders. Turn the body 51

Right: Turning the trunk to the inside, with arms outstretched.

from the waist until one hand is pointing to the horse's ears and the other to the tail. Keep the arms at the same height and an equal weight on both seat bones. The head should be turned to look at each hand as it points to the back of the horse.

6 Bend the upper body forward until the chest lies along the top of the horse's neck. Swing the arms backwards and up as far as they will go. This will also help to loosen the waist and back.

7 Swing the legs, keeping them as long as possible, one forward and the other back. This helps when giving canter aids, especially when learning flying changes and then tempi changes.

There are many other exercises that will improve relaxation and suppleness, such as rotating the ankles and the wrists. They should all be carried out with a good rhythm and, if done when the horse is moving, in rhythm with the horse's steps.

A competition rider should remember that there is a mark at the end of each dressage test for the position of the rider and the correct application of the aids. It is worth spending some time on making your position as perfect as possible so that the aids can be given in a seemingly effortless way and the complete picture is one of harmony and elegance as well as being seen to be effective.

Left: A correct, relaxed position.

53

CHAPTER 4

EARLY RIDING

A newly broken horse trotting calmly and freely forward.

The early training of the young horse under saddle starts as soon as he is accepting the rider's weight and can walk, trot and canter off the lunge round an enclosed area without becoming anxious or tense. The rider is now in charge. Before this stage has been reached, the horse has learned to carry a person in the saddle while still on the lunge, and the trainer holding the lunge line and carrying the whip has been the one to be obeyed. As the time approaches for the horses to be ridden loose, he must have adapted to the voice of the rider for halt, walk and trot and must feel happy with a light contact from the rider's hands and legs.

The horse adopting a rounder outline. At the beginning of training, the horse's weight is more on his forehand and the hind legs are not engaged, so when a young horse is first ridden his point of balance will be further forward. A general purpose or jumping saddle is used at this stage, to enable the rider to remain in balance with the horse.

Leg contact and aids

It is vital that the horse learns to accept the leg aids and the weight of the legs against his sides in his early training. Initially, the first person to sit on a young horse will keep their legs well forward and quiet, but every day the leg position must become more established so that the leg can be used in the correct way and in the right place, i.e. approximately a hand's width behind the girth, so that the horse will learn to move forward from a small inward nudge with the lower legs in this position. With a forward-going, sensitive Thoroughbred, it is often unnecessary to use the leg as this type of horse frequently powers forward under his own nervous energy; it is not until the time comes to teach him leg-yielding that it becomes apparent that this horse has not learnt to accept the leg contact at all, and there can be quite a rebellion over yielding to the leg under such circumstances.

55

A more advanced horse in working trot, showing balance and engagement.

Rein contact and aids

The same criteria apply to the acceptance of the hand. It is all too easy to ride a sensitive horse with the rein too light. If this is the case, although he will learn to turn, circle and stop, he will not learn to work through the rein and develop his paces to their utmost because he has not been offered the correct weight of rein from the beginning. The rider monitors the weight of rein. When the horse is working in proper self-carriage, the rein should become light as a result. The rein should not be light because the horse is backing off the rider's hand. The more advanced the training, the lighter the horse should become to the rider's hand.

Because it is so important to offer the horse a good feel in the initial stages of his training, the rider must be experienced and have a secure and established position. A novice rider is

not able to teach a young horse to accept a contact without resistance.

The rider must be able to feel the texture in the mouth and develop an elastic connection that follows the movement of the head and neck at all times. The allowing hand must let the horse take the connection forward and down and encourage the young horse to work forward in a round outline with his nose in front of the vertical and without restricting him or holding him in a frame. Initially, the young horse will want to move his head and neck to balance himself as he learns to move round the schooling area and he must have the confidence to do this without any restriction on his mouth from the rider. At this stage, the downward transitions from trot to walk and walk to halt are carried out by the rider restraining the forward movement with a 'non-allowing' hand, together with the vocal commands that the horse has already learned

Loosening up in canter, with the rider's seat out of the saddle to give the horse more freedom to use his back. This rider's stirrups are too long for this exercise, causing the heels to be drawn up and the lower leg to go too far back.

to obey on the lunge. The voice is omitted as the horse learns to accept the rider's aids.

Later on, this 'non-allowing' rein is used to contain the impulsion created by the rider and to establish the half-halt. Whenever the hand is used in a non-allowing way, and for whatever reason, even if it is because the horse is being naughty, the quality of the contact must remain. This quality and elastic feeling come from relaxed and supple elbows and shoulders. It is actually the shoulders that allow. If you take approximately 680–900 g (1½–2lb) weight in each rein, it is easier to feel if your shoulders are relaxed and allowing than if you are cautiously trying to be too light in your contact and letting tension creep into your hands. When the horse has truly accepted the contact and is working through the rein, the weight will vary slightly but it should be the aim of all aspiring top riders to maintain a good texture and quality of

Loosening up in trot. The horse is round but not taking the hand forward and down sufficiently.

contact. If the young horse draws back from your hand, always check the quality of contact you are offering him. The hand must be still and quiet to the horse's mouth but must also follow the movement. A still hand with rigid arms will block all movement, as will hands that move excessively with the rider's body.

The influence of the rider's weight

The third thing that must be correct from the beginning, along with the contact of the leg and the hand, is the rider's weight. After a few weeks the young horse should be familiar with the rider's weight and it is important that this weight on his back should help and not hinder him to fulfil what is being asked of him.

Later on, as training progresses, the rider's weight has an

A correct outline for a working trot.

important supportive role to play when used in conjunction with the rein and leg aids. In the beginning, however, until the horse's back has strengthened sufficiently, the rider must sit lightly and help the horse by always bringing their weight to the inside on turns and circles, as if riding a bicycle but without actually leaning over. The rider who sits to the outside of a circle will make a young horse extremely uncomfortable as well as unbalanced.

To sit lightly on a young horse, the rider should have the stirrups slightly shorter than usual and, without moving the position of the lower legs, nor actually taking their seat out of the saddle, incline the upper body marginally forward so that the weight feels as if it is no longer on the seat bones but is transferred to the knee and thigh. This will relieve pressure on the horse's back until it is strong enough to carry the rider in a normal dressage seat.

Obedience

Having established these basic requirements, it is now time to proceed with the actual training itself and the horse's acceptance of the aids.

Nothing can be accomplished until the young horse is obedient. Care must be taken that he understands everything that is being asked of him and, in this, each horse must be treated as an individual and given time to mature according to his own ability to progress and accept the work. It is most important that the young horse is physically able to do what is wanted and is not made sour or anxious because too much has been asked of him during the first few months, before his muscles are sufficiently developed to cope with the rider's weight. It is better that the young horse is ridden by an experienced light-weight rider at this stage.

During the early stages, and definitely if the horse is only three years old, the emphasis must be on riding freely forward and on promoting the obedience, confidence and relaxation of the horse before any change to his outline is sought. From the beginning, the horse must be encouraged to take the hand forward and down, stretching the neck and loosening the back muscles, which always tighten when the rider first gets on, especially with a young and weak back.

With the young horse it is advisable to allow as much freedom as possible in the walk. He should be given a long rein so that his natural walk steps are not interfered with through a contact on the mouth and he is allowed to swing forward using his head and neck in the natural way that he would without a rider on his back. Any restriction or tension that occurs in the walk steps at this stage, due to an insensitive approach or ignorance on the part of the rider, can do untold damage that may never be remedied, so that we finish up with an incorrect gait entirely due to rider mismanagement. While walking, is essential that the rider's legs remain quietly in contact with the horse's sides and are kept still unless giving an aid. A lazy horse will become totally oblivious to the leg if the rider nags continually with it and therefore it is important to carry a schooling whip when riding and idle horse, to back up the leg aid and encourage the horse to walk forward with long rhythmic steps from the very beginning. With a tense horse, that walks too fast, the leg should still remain quietly in contact and any temptation to draw the leg away from the horse's sides should be avoided as even more tension will then develop when the leg has to be used. The 'hot' horse will eventually become quieter when he has learnt to accept the rider's leg lying gently against his sides.

Care must also be taken that the rider's arm is relaxed and follows the movement, albeit with a long rein. If the arms are stiff and fixed, the horse may come up against a jar on his mouth as he nods forward, which will stop him nodding correctly and thus shorten the steps so that the first unwanted seed of 'backing off the rein' will have been sown. When making the first transitions from walk to halt, a soft contact is sought on the mouth, which gradually restrains the forward movement without pulling back. The wrists and arms remain relaxed and sympathetic and at the same time the voice is used in a similar manner as it was when lungeing the horse. When the horse understands this first rein aid, used in conjunction with the voice, the voice can gradually be omitted.

During the first few months of training, the attitude to the leg aids is very important as, without sufficient respect and a generous, 'forward-thinking' response to an inward nudge from within the leg contact, the horse will gradually learn to work only under his own terms and will resent or ignore demands to increase activity when required.

Inevitably, there will also come a time when the horse is genuinely frightened of some object or has a disinclination to leave other horses or even his own stable yard. If he has not already learnt to respect and obey the leg and rein aids, a disobedience will occur that could lead to napping. It is important to avoid this sort of situation and to keep the young horse in an enclosed and familiar place or school until he is

Walking above the bit with a loose rein contact.

sufficiently disciplined to stop and start in walk, trot and canter, to be slowed down if his speed increases beyond a reasonably safe level and to turn in either direction when asked.

Hacking out

The young horse should only be hacked out when the rider feels that the basic methods of control have been established. If a bird in the hedge startles the horse and he canters off, the rider must be able to circle and stop without the situation getting out of hand. An old and sensible horse is ideal to take out as a companion for a youngster. If the young horse has an upset, the old horse can be halted and have a calming influence or lead the way in a spooky place.

A horse in a medium walk, accepting the rein contact.

It is good to get the young horse out as much as possible until he develops some muscles and grows stronger. Work on circles in the school will be very tiring in his early training and it is important that the bones, joints and tendons are not subjected to too much stress if the horse is going to endure when we eventually train him to an advanced standard. Learning to walk up and down hills, splashing through water and trotting through the woods and fields is a perfect way to accustom the horse to the rider's weight and to teach him to be obedient to the simple demands of the rein and legs aids. Only short distances of rising trot should be asked for until the horse becomes fitter, and so you should introduce many transitions during the riding out time. Always reward the horse with your voice and a pat when things are done well.

Obviously, it is not everybody's good fortune to have ideal

Stretching the neck down for a free walk on a long rein. The tension in the neck will disappear if the neck is allowed to go forward a bit more.

hacking country for a young horse so, if you live on a busy road, all the early work will have to be done in an arena. Use as large a space as possible so that you can work on straight lines and not just continuous circling. Work for short periods only, until the horse is strong and, when possible, transport him to a venue from where he can be introduced to the countryside in safety. All competition horses have to get used to travelling and taking a young horse out quietly in a horsebox

with another horse is a good way to start the procedure and prepare the horse for his first competition.

Confidence/reward/punishment

Through the basic training of the young horse, we wish to create a good foundation for his further education. At this early stage, he must gain confidence in the rider and be obedient at all times so that he learns to work in a relaxed way and therefore uses his body properly as he develops the appropriate muscles and carries himself in all gaits. He must also learn to accept and carry the rider without losing his athleticism. The rider must be aware at all times of 'the feel' they expect from the horse, must know exactly what they are aiming for, and be absolutely clear in their aids and fair to the horse so that the horse is not left guessing what is wanted.

The subject of punishment and reward has been discussed and practised ever since Xenophon wrote his *Art of Horsemanship* in 400 BC. However much one wishes to train the horse through explanation and goodwill, however careful and patient the trainer is, sooner or later it will be realized that all training is a matter of reward and punishment in which the horse must learn two things:

1   If he does not obey a light aid, a stronger aid will be use and if he indulges in anti-social behaviour (bucking, rearing or kicking), he will be punished.
2   Obeying the rider can be a pleasurable experience.

Punishment should be used as infrequently as possible and never because of loss of temper on the part of the rider. 'Force without thought' is, at all times, to be avoided. The voice, the spur, and the stick can all be used in varying degrees to signify the rider's displeasure at the horse's disobedience. The horse must learn as soon as possible that, if the leg aid has been ignored, a slight flick from a dressage whip in the area of the leg, means: 'Why are you not listening? I asked you to go forward.' This procedure must be strictly adhered to, to keep the horse 'in front of the leg' and not let him become idle in his work. However, if he is being positively nappy, an experienced rider must use the stick on the hind quarters as a serious punishment.

The spurs can be used to reinforce an ignored leg aid but the aid must initially be given with the lower leg alone and then reinforced with the spur without the leg position being altered. Spurs should not be used on a very young horse. He must be made to listen to the lower leg in conjunction with the voice and a flick of the whip. Spurs can be used in a severe way to punish a horse but the dressage whip is more effective and does less damage to the skin and muscles. Sharp spurs can break the skin while blunt spurs will bruise the muscles. A horse's pain threshold is extremely high and it is not good to make a horse dead to the spur through overuse or misuse, neither of which can be considered good horsemanship.

An angry or tense horse will often hold its breath. If a confrontation has been unavoidable or necessary for some reason, once the horse has 'given in' it is advisable to wait in halt until he has relaxed sufficiently to take a deep breath before continuing with the work. It is a good idea to work on an easy exercise after doing something new or difficult.

The voice can, and must, be used to express pleasure with work well done and if a good relationship has developed the horse will soon learn when he is being praised or being grumbled at. Punishing the horse by jagging at his mouth in a temper is never to be condoned.

If the horse ignores the rein aid, he must be restrained in a very positive manner and, as soon as he yields to the pressure, the hand must be given back in a soft way so that he realizes his mouth is more comfortable if he is obedient. If this procedure is strictly adhered to, the horse will soon learn not to pull against the rider's hand and will give in his jaw. The concept is spoiled by a rider who takes hold of the horse strongly, instead of insisting that he becomes obedient so that the rein can then be lightened to an acceptable weight. A rider who is not in balance is not able to make these adjustments to the contact with the horse's mouth and it is a grave offence to keep in balance using the reins for support and thus ruining the feel on the horse's mouth. Always make a point of finishing a schooling session with something easy that can be done well so that the horse goes back to the stable having been rewarded and in a calm and happy state of mind.

CHAPTER 5

BASIC SCHOOLING

When the horse is strong enough to undertake a longer daily session in the school, usually sometime during his fourth year, the time has come to develop the outline for the working paces, to establish rhythm in these paces and to confirm the acceptance of the rein and the leg aids in order to produce a supple, obedient and fairly well-balanced young horse.

I say 'fairly-well balanced', because, at this stage, many horses have not yet finished growing; they are certainly not well muscled and are often stronger in front than they are behind, which adds to the difficulty of transferring their weight to their hindquarters and engaging their hind legs. They may still be unable to control their own natural impulsion with a rider's weight on their back. All these difficulties will be appreciated by a sympathetic and understanding trainer. I have seen many potentially excellent horses ruined by riders who have been too ambitious and overhasty about establishing balance and achieving what they think of as an advanced self-carriage at the expense of quality and confidence.

Loosening-up

All horses must be allowed plenty of time to loosen-up before they are asked to do anything in the way of work. Most horses will have been standing in a stable for at least sixteen hours before they are ridden. Even if they are turned out for a few hours each day, it is usually after work. I thoroughly approve of this routine but that does not alter the fact that movement is limited in a stable and, therefore, a loosening-up period prior to more active exercise is a necessity that must be undertaken by the horse exactly as it would be by a human gymnast, dancer or any other athlete.

Some young horses are best put on the lunge to loosen them

A young horse trotting freely forward but not round enough to engage from behind.

up, especially after a day off. Any horses who come out of the stable in an exuberant manner are better to let off steam on the lunge before being ridden. It is impossible to school a horse if he is too fresh and if this happens often, thought must be given to whether he is being fed strictly according to the work that he is being asked to do. He may be turned out each day to keep him calm and relaxed. Even with a calm, laid-back individual, I like to have him led around for five minutes before I get on and then, having mounted and tightened the girth, I walk him for a further five to ten minutes on a loose rein. This gives the horse plenty of time to look around and settle down in the area where he is to be worked.

When the horse is being led in hand, he should walk in a

calm manner without pulling on the reins. If pulling does occur, it is better if he is led in a headcollar or lunge cavesson as bad habits in the mouth can be formed that would be undesirable when being ridden, for example, too much pulling on one side of the mouth by the person on the ground, could cause head tipping and an excessive bend in the neck. A 'hard', as opposed to an 'elastic', feeling on the tongue and bars of the mouth will then develop and, because of this, a young horse will get into the habit of drawing back his tongue and pressing down on the rider's hand.

The next stage in the loosening-up process is to ask the horse to trot forward and encourage the stretching-down outline that has been established on the lunge over the last few months. The difference now is that he must learn to take the rider's hand forward and down with confidence. Once this procedure had been accomplished, the horse is far less likely to drop behind the bit, overbend or work just 'behind the vertical' during the more advanced work that he will do later on, than if the stretching down with the hand has been omitted from the early training.

There are two situations when I would not work a horse long and low. The first is when he has an excessive amount of natural impulsion which pushes him too much onto 'front wheel drive', so to speak. This usually makes him break in the neck behind the fourth or fifth vertebra, causing him to muscle-up in the neck in the wrong way. We are aiming to develop the neck muscles in front of the withers, not those at the top of the neck behind the poll. If the horse is over-impulsioned, he will not stretch down in a relaxed way nor loosen his back as required. When a horse comes out with this much energy, it is better to let him stretch after he has done some work, when he has less energy and can benefit from the exercise.

The second instance is when the horse is abnormally on his forehand and so unbalanced that to put his neck down long and low would only aggravate the situation. I would not choose a horse with this problem for pure dressage, but such horses can often jump extremely well and therefore have to be schooled for eventing dressage. The stretching down is not included in the training programme of such horses to any great extent, and more emphasis is put on acquiring better balance and less weight on the forehand from the beginning. They should be given the opportunity to stretch the neck and take the hand forward at various intervals during a training session but not for too long a period and not until they can

The horse starting to take the hand forward and down but still falling on to his forehand at this stage.

do so without leaning and supporting themselves on the rider's hand.

Rhythm

Rhythm is the direct beat of the footfalls on the ground within the jurisdiction of the gait. Tempo is the speed of the rhythm. Having stretched the topline and loosened the muscles in the neck and back the horse should settle into his own natural rhythm in trot. Our aim during the early training is to improve and establish this rhythm and produce a good working trot.

Do not develop an obsession about the horse being on the

bit at this stage. The young horse should never be forced into a 'frame' or position by a strong and dictatorial rein. He must be given time to work from behind into the hand, and encouraged to adopt the shape that is required for the working paces. At this stage of training, when the shape is not yet established, the most usual problems are:

1 The horse that likes to hollow and carry his head and neck too high. In this case I like to work with the horse very round and deep and it would be immaterial at this stage if the poll was not the highest point.
2 The horse that has a tendency to 'curl up', or 'roll over', as it is called when he rounds his neck too much and brings the front line of his nose behind the vertical. This horse should not be worked as deep as the first one but must be encouraged to take the hand forward with a longer neck and the poll a little higher. The main aim is to get the horse round throughout his whole body but, according to each horse's own particular problems, there will be variations at the start of the training.

If the lunge work has been done correctly, the horse will not be hollow but it is more than likely that he will not willingly consent to accept your hand, so great care must be taken to offer him a connection that is comfortable and acceptable.

Try to keep the work as simple as possible, with the horse concentrating and responding well to the aids. Start making trot to walk transitions from rising trot. If these are not immediately obeyed, go back and ask for walk to halt until the horse is more attentive. In between the halt transitions, walk with the reins loose so that the walk steps do not become shortened.

The emphasis is still on riding freely forward but the young horse must slow down obediently when required so that the weight of the rein can be adjusted and the horse never learns to lean on the rider's hand. You will never achieve balance without obedience.

The horse must be ridden forward at a speed that develops his natural rhythm, but not so fast that it causes him to flatten and run with short steps. This is called 'pushing the horse out of his stride' and if it happens the rider must adjust the pace to re-establish the rhythm.

At first the young horse will have difficulty in maintaining a consistent rhythm when he changes direction in the school and therefore, at the start, it is better to work on a large circle on the horse's easy side – usually the left rein. First ask

Improved balance and a rounder outline.

for smooth transitions from trot to walk and walk to trot. When you are pleased with the work on this rein, change the rein in walk and proceed in the same way on a right-hand circle.

Gradually, as the rhythm is established and the horse becomes used to a good connection, he will accept the hand and come into a round outline. If he powers forward too much, loses his balance, and leans on the rider's hands he must be slowed down so that the rider can readjust their weight and the horse's balance and ride forward again with the rein lighter. This adjustment may have to be made very frequently, until the horse begins to get the idea of carrying himself without supporting his head and neck on the rider's hand and hardening his jaw on the bit. These are the first steps towards learning the half-halt.

Bending and turning

One difficulty with young horses, especially of the hot-blooded type, is that they are very easily distracted and will throw their heads up and hollow if another horse comes into the school or if they are disturbed by a noise, etc. This habit must not be allowed to establish itself. To overcome it, you can 'show him the way down', to being round again with the inside rein by bending him onto a smaller circle. In this way he will learn to bend his neck when so directed, and the bending will regain his attention and soften his neck, which usually becomes rather tense when the horse hollows. Be sure to allow the bend to the inside by releasing the outside pressure on the mouth, allowing the neck to stretch but not entirely losing connection. Later on, the horse must learn to bend while accepting a contact on the outside rein, but not in the beginning. At this stage, it is enough that he learns to allow his neck to be softened by being pliable and that he 'gives' in the jaw, lowers his head and neck and is rewarded by the rider's hand softening and giving to him. At the same time as this bend is being asked for, the inside leg must be pressed against the horse's side by the girth to stop the shoulder falling in with too much weight on it. It is important to encourage the horse to bend round the leg, rather than 'fall in', making the circle too small.

Initially, the rein aids used to ask the horse to turn are not the easiest for him to learn and accept. It is essential that the rider's weight is used by increasing the pressure down onto the inside stirrup to indicate the direction and make it easier for the horse to comply, as in riding a bicycle. At the same time, the inside rein should be drawn away from the neck – an opening rein – to show him the way he has to go. The outside rein must be kept in a fairly low position to prevent the neck from bending too much. If the neck does bend excessively, the shoulders will not come round onto the turn. At the same time, the horse must be ridden forward very purposefully making sure the rein contact is 'allowing'. The rider must look at a point in the school to which they would like to go and then make sure that they get there. When a young horse is first let loose in the school with a rider on board, it is helpful to have somebody on the ground holding a lunge whip. The horse will have been conditioned to this while being lunged and so the trainer on the ground can still help to urge the horse forward if necessary while he is learning to be steered.

Gradually, as the horse learns what is wanted, the opening rein can be changed to an indication on the inside rein, with a slight increase of weight in the hand, along with the rider's weight placed to the inside, as already mentioned, and backed up by their inside leg. The turns and circles will improve quickly as long as they are not made too difficult and are executed at the correct speed – not too fast, for then the horse loses balance; not so slow that he loses the rhythm.

Establishing the aids for canter

It is advisable to establish a good rhythm in the working trot and be able to steer the horse on 20-m (66-ft) circles, across the diagonal and to be able to turn left and right when required before starting to canter. Cantering can be the cause of tension and excitement and a certain amount of control is necessary, so leave cantering to the last half of the daily training session if it excites the young horse.

Below and right: A novice horse cantering with the off-fore as the leading leg. The near hind has taken all the weight before the off-hind and the near-fore step on to the ground together. The off-fore is about to go forward to complete the stride before the moment of suspension shown in the picture on the right, with the near-hind then coming to the ground to start the sequence of steps again. Note

how far the off-hind steps under the body. This is a huge step that has pushed the rider up from the horse's back in spite of adopting a light seat. The rider has stiffened slightly against the movement causing the arms to become rather straight and unallowing. In the picture below the seat is lower to the saddle and the arms are now softer.

It is easier for the young horse to canter on a circle as he is naturally bent to the leading leg, and a correct strike-off is more likely to happen if it is asked for on a curve. In the early stages, the rider must adopt a light seat to free the horse's back so that he does not feel inhibited about moving forward into canter. The rider's weight must be to the inside of the horse, the inside leg used on the girth and the outside leg a little behind the girth at the same time as the voice is used to encourage the canter strike-off. The horse should be familiar with cantering on the lunge and so should obey the voice. When the horse does canter for the first time, he should be well rewarded with the voice and patted when he is brought back to trot. It does not matter which leg he leads on at the beginning, but if he is asked on a corner and the rider's weight is correct it is more than likely that he will strike-off correctly. He must associate going into canter with the rider's outside leg going back and will very soon learn what this aid means. It will become obvious after several sessions which leading

leg the horse favours in canter and it is more tactful to ask for canter on the easier lead to start with. When he has become more settled on that side, then ask on the more difficult rein.

When cantering, it is important to follow the movement of the head and neck with the arms and not restrict the natural nod that the young horse makes. If the horse is forced to canter with a restraining, unallowing hand, the three beats of the canter and the moment of suspension will be inhibited and the gait can be spoilt, in as much as a flat canter, with no moment of suspension, is likely to develop. The young horse usually canters too fast and will learn to set his jaw against the rein if not allowed the freedom he needs to move his head and neck. The canter should not be slowed down too much at first. Instead, bring the horse back to trot frequently and canter again when the balance has been restored. Eventually, the canter will settle down to the horse's natural rhythm in this gait and, as he becomes familiar with cantering on either leg on demand, the canter can then be gradually developed.

The horse must be cantered if this gait is to be developed. Do not avoid canter work because the horse finds it difficult. It is desirable that the canter work should improve at roughly the same rate as the improvement of the trot work, otherwise the weaker of the two gaits will lower the standard of competition results when you reach this stage of training. If the cantering is ignored, this progression will not be equal, so cantering the horse is a necessary and important part of the daily training routine, whether on the lunge or under saddle, The trot work will also improve the cantering, in as much as, when more contained impulsion is manageable in the trot, this will also be reflected in the canter. The acceptance of the hand and the roundness will show similar progress, albeit to a minor degree.

Relaxation and straightness

Having discussed aspects of the very basic walk, trot and canter and some of the problems that may be encountered, this is now a suitable point to consider how to develop them into the working gaits that are required in the Novice tests and are also the foundation for all further training.

Running through this system of training, are several objectives that must be considered on a daily basis as well as in a long-term policy. As already mentioned, first and foremost the horse must be obedient. Nothing can be achieved unless there is a confident and willing submission to the demands of the

Working trot showing good steps but the horse is not in a rounded outline.

rider. Added to this is a priority of forward movement, which, over months and years will slowly be channelled into producing the most rhythmical and impressive work of which the horse is capable.

Relaxation is a major factor in achieving the desired working trot and canter. Relaxation means mental calmness as well as the softness and pliability of the muscles. Without relaxation there can be no suppleness, no flexion in the jaw, no proper control of impulsion and, therefore, no 'cadenced' gaits. Cadence can be described as an energetic, springy way of going that adds charisma and expression to the gaits.

Without relaxation, it will be impossible to straighten the horse in order to improve him. If he is straightened by force, creating stiffness in his muscles, he will not develop the swing and use of the body that is vital to his way of going and may develop a tendency to tip his head.

All horses have a stiff and less-athletic side. Most untrained horses are crooked even before being broken-in, due to a number of factors such as possible 'genetic handedness' and always being led from the near side, so that, from being a foal onwards, a curve is developed in the neck and the muscles on the outside of the neck are conditioned to stretch while those on the inside are not.

When being lunged or ridden, the line of the track on which the horse is moving should be matched by the line of his spine through the centre of his body. When he is on a straight line, there should be no bend in the neck nor any deviation of the shoulder or hindquarters from that line. When he is on a circle, whether large or small, the outside hind foot should follow the track of the outside front foot, unless it is deliberately being asked to do otherwise.

The ability to straighten the horse is something that must be established easily and as soon as possible during the early training. However, patience is the key to this problem and nothing can be achieved through force or irritation on the part of the rider. As a result of losing balance, weight will be thrown onto one or other of the shoulders, producing a deviation from the line and a crooked horse. This syndrome will be prominent to a greater or lesser degree throughout the whole training to Grand Prix level. Unless the horse is straight, he cannot truly work through from behind, engaging the hindquarters, and come up in the shoulders, so maintaining a classically advanced position. He has to be straightened, or positioned, before such exercises as leg-yielding, walk pirouettes, medium and extended trot and canter as well as being bent round the rider's inside leg in shoulder-in and half-pass. All this must be established before the tempo changes, canter pirouettes, piaffe and basic passage that make up the advanced work. However, much can be done in the early stages that will prepare for the more refined work later on.

Straightness and engagement will improve together. The looser and more correct the horse becomes, the more he straightness himself and the easier he will find it to work and engage from behind.

As the rein contact is established, it is easy to feel which side of the horse has a tendency to harden and does not yield and soften, especially when walking on a small circle. On the side that feels more spongy, the neck develops too much bend, with the result that the shoulders fall out away from the curve in the neck. It is a very slow process to encourage the muscles on the bendy, soft side to stretch so that the horse willingly takes the rider's hand forward and down while keeping his neck straight.

After riding the horse forward and being able to control

the pace, the next most important item on the training agenda is to straighten first the neck and then the whole horse.

Some horses are too flexible or rubbery in their necks, usually more so to one side. Others are extremely stiff and give the impression of never being able to put their heads to right or left under any circumstances. The stiff neck usually associates with a stiff back and to deal with this problem I like, first of all, to bend the neck very gently and slowly, in halt, to one side and then the other, with much patting and praising when it can be accomplished without moving the feet. Then walk forward and ask for a bend in a like manner while moving along the wall of the arena, making sure to do the exercise equally on both reins.

It is worth remembering that a bend is of no value if it cannot be straightened out, while a straight horse, albeit a stiff one, is of no value if it cannot be bent.

Another point to remember, when thinking about straightness, is that the neck and shoulders have to be positioned and controlled first and then the horse ridden forward with energy from the hindquarters. It is not sufficient to try to line up the quarters with the shoulders, as then the forehand will not be under the rider's influence and will, therefore, still generate problems when you endeavour to keep the horse on a straight or curved line without deviation.

When suppleness and relaxation, rhythm, contact on the bit, along with response to the aids, and straightness have all been mastered and established, start asking the horse to work with more impulsion, i.e. to 'jump more' or 'come more from behind', both expressions meaning that the energy generated must be channelled into making the horse taller under the rider, with the steps coming higher off the ground and so obtaining more collection.

Collection is not asked for in the young horse. At four years old the horse works at Novice level, which only involves working paces. At five years old a small amount of shortening and collection is asked for mostly in trot in the Elementary standard tests. It is not until Medium level that collection has to be shown. A very talented young horse can be pushed through the lower standard tests and achieve Medium work at a tender age, but it is unwise to put too much pressure on young joints if you want your horse to endure.

The young novice horse has now learnt to walk, trot and canter round the school, to make basic transitions in and out of all three gaits and to turn and circle when asked.

The rider has a clear idea of what their aims are and what aspects of training to focus on to achieve the desired result.

When the horse has been worked on the lunge and lightly under saddle for a few months, he should have begun to develop the correct muscles along his back, especially behind the saddle, and also at the shoulder end of the neck in front of the wither. The muscles on the forearms and forelegs will usually develop long before the corresponding ones between the hock and the stifle on the hind legs. However, as the horse is encouraged to work with more power from behind, and as the hind legs step further under the body, the hind legs will also muscle-up.

The trainer must be patient while the young horse develops and whatever time is necessary must be given to allow the horse to become stronger. If too much work is done on a weak horse he will:

1 grow to dislike the work;
2 stiffen to save himself from the discomfort;
3 develop unlevelness in his gaits which may never be put right – usually most noticeable in the walk;
4 not learn to balance himself correctly;
5 he may have a permanently weak back as he will not have learnt how to use it.

Working through the rein

As and when the horse matures, more consideration must be given to the contact and the outline so that, eventually, he works 'on the bit'.

A horse is 'on the bit' when he is accepting the rider's hand and maintains the outline that is suitable for his stage of training. The rider should have a good feel on the horse's mouth but his feel must include the sensation of the whole horse moving through his body and not only concentrate on the feeling down the rein. The hind legs must be stepping under a certain amount, otherwise the horse will not have the necessary balance to give this good feeling. If the horse leans on the hand, the rider must use transitions and half-halts to lighten the contact, otherwise the horse will get used to leaning. Usually, the rider will have to slow the horse down to lighten the rein and encourage him to balance himself. If the hand is being accepted properly, the horse's nose should be slightly in front of the vertical and the outline will be consistent and without resistance.

At the start of training, the young horse will not stay on the bit for long periods of time and he should be rewarded for performing a few circles in balance, without resistance, by the rider making a transition to walk and patting him. When you get an improvement, try to consolidate it so that you can repeat the work in the same way. When you are training, you must be prepared to improve one thing at the expense of something else, albeit temporarily. For example, with a young horse it is possible that calmness will disappear when obedience is insisted upon. However, the horse must be obedient and so he must be schooled in such a way that it is very clear what is wanted. When he complies, he must be rewarded immediately, so that he gets over the tensions and calmly obeys the rider.

A clever horse will soon notice if the rider stops asking a difficult question when he gets cross and tense and will use this to his advantage. It is important, therefore, to stop asking the question only when you get a good result, not when you are faced with tension, otherwise tension becomes part of an evasion and the horse's attitude to learning will be corrupted.

In the beginning, it is also likely that the quality that has been achieved in the rein and also in the horse's balance will be rather fragile, so that these two desired results of training can disappear very easily when the horse is first asked to lengthen his stride, make sideways steps or even to straighten. He should still be rewarded for attempting to perform any new exercise. With time he will be able to do the exercise with fluency and ease and the quality will return.

As work progresses, all the training should slot together, with the horse and rider working in harmony to improve the exercises that have been learnt over the years.

CHAPTER 6

WORKING AT NOVICE LEVEL

A young horse showing active lengthened strides in trot. The rein contact is a little insecure.

A horse that is ready to compete at Novice level must have a confirmed outline in working trot and canter, be able to show lengthened strides in those gaits, keep the same outline while making transitions within the pace and perform medium walk, walk on a long rein, halt and a few steps of rein-back.

The time taken to achieve the necessary standard will vary considerably from horse to horse. A talented, naturally

Above: The same horse giving a perfect example of taking the rein forward and down and stretching his top line.

Right: A young horse lengthening in a more balanced way.

83

coordinated four-year-old can win at Novice level, while a less-mature, or very large, animal will still be struggling within the confines of a 20 x 40-m (66 x 130-ft) arena when he is five or six years old, especially if his career in dressage training was not begun as early as it might have been.

Working the horse in a round outline

It is necessary for the rider to be able to encourage the horse to readjust to a round outline if, for some reason, he has hollowed or stiffened and lost the desired position. When a horse hollows in his outline, he will lift his head too high, using the muscles under the neck and setting his jaw, drop his shoulders and dip his back, hunching up his hindquarters and putting weight on his forehand. The usual reasons for doing this are:

1 Excitement, tension and overfreshness.
2 A non-acceptance of the hand, usually more pronounced on one side.

A novice horse in a better balance and taking the rider's hand forward.

3 The rider giving a leg aid without having a secure leg contact and so surprising or startling a sensitive horse.
4 The rider asking the horse to do something that he has not been prepared for and does not understand.
5 The horse being distracted by an outside influence and using this as an evasion to avoid submission.
6 Physical weakness.

When any of these difficulties arise, they are more likely to result in a prolonged problem if the horse has set his jaw on the stiff side of his body,thus making it impossible for the rider to keep an even contact and straighten out the crookedness that will have occurred. Under these circumstances, it is likely that the horse will not take the contact forward on the soft and hollow side and, in some cases, will not allow any connection on that side without an excessive bend in the neck developing.

The first reaction from the rider must be to obtain an even contact by persuading the horse to accept the lighter rein and not hold so much on the stronger side for the horse to set against.

A novice horse hollowing against the hand as he goes into a canter.

85

Right: Showing a slight bend round the rider's inside leg as she turns on to a left-hand circle.

Below: Continuing to show a pleasing and relaxed outline on the circle.

There are many ways of encouraging the horse to re-establish a round outline. The easiest way to do this is to work on a large circle to the stiff side (usually the right side), then gradually ease the head and neck to an inside position and then ease off the pressure on the strong rein so that the horse feels more contact on the left side (in this case the outside rein) and becomes familiar with taking this hand forward. At the beginning, the horse will only manage a few steps before reverting to bending to the left once more. He must repeatedly be made straight again with the inside rein before making this softer and lighter as often as possible. The inside leg should be used sufficiently to prevent the circle becoming too small. Always start on a 20-m (66-ft) circle. After a few circles, the horse should get used to the idea of accepting an even contact and stay out on the large circle and should also begin to re-establish the roundness that had been lost.

The ability to perform good circles is one of the most important tests throughout the training. To be able to achieve this at Novice level, the horse must not only be even in the rein, he must also listen to the rider's leg in a more advanced way. He has learnt to go forward from the leg whenever requested but he must now yield to the leg so that the leg can help to prevent his shoulder falling in on turns and circles and his hindquarters deviating to the outside. Leg pressure on the girth will help to control the shoulders and leg pressure slightly behind the girth will control the quarters.

Leg-yielding

Leg-yielding is the simplest of all lateral movements and it can be used to help to straighten the horse and obtain an even contact on the mouth long before shoulder-in has been mastered.

When the horse has learnt to yield to the leg, the leg will then be effective in preventing the shoulders falling in on circles and turns. It does not take long for the horse to learn to move away from pressure applied next to the girth with the inside leg, especially if he has been taught to move away from the stick when being lunged, as described in Chapter 3.

Leg-yielding is useful if the horse is inclined to set on the right rein and has to be persuaded to take more connection on the left side. As well as positioning him on a circle, as already described, in order to ease off the strong contact, another useful way to do this and to introduce leg-yielding, is to follow the track round the arena on the right rein and,

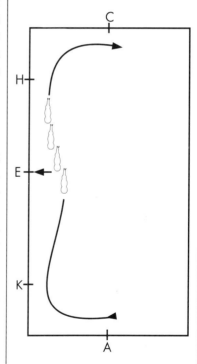

The first exercise in leg-yielding. Leave the track for a few metres and then push the horse back to the track.

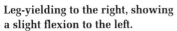

Leg-yielding to the right, showing a slight flexion to the left.

A correct leg-yield to the right

when going up the long side, make a shallow loop in from the track. When the point opposite X is reached where, normally, the line would be ridden back to the end of the long side, keep the horse parallel to the long side, straight in the neck, and ask for a few steps of leg-yield to the left. Horses always like to draw back to the track so it is a good idea to ask for the first sideways steps in a direction in which he would like to go, as opposed to leaving the track, which he would find more difficult. Even putting the quarters or the shoulder in from the track in a leg-yielding position can be quite a difficult obedience exercise for a young horse.

When leg-yielding, the horse should be straight from head to tail with a very slight flexion, i.e. putting his head sideways from the joint between the head and the neck at the poll. He should move forward and sideways from the rider's inside leg and must learn to cross over with the inside fore and hind steps as he does so.

When first starting this basic lateral movement and using it, as in this instance, to get the horse more into the left or outside rein, I advise using the same aids to push the horse onto the left shoulder as well as into the contact in the left hand. This involves asking for more flexion and bend than in classical leg-yielding but serves the purpose of stretching the muscles on the soft side of the horse and softening and bending him on the hard, stiff side. When this bending and yielding to the leg has been established, the rein can be given away on the hard side so that the horse gets used to accepting the softer rein only. This will help to even up the contact and get the horse round.

The exercises can be done for a short time in walk and then in a slow, relaxed trot. When the horse yields to the leg and stays round, he can then be asked to perform leg-yielding in a good working trot from the centre line to the track, along the sides of the wall or across the diagonal.

The aids for leg-yielding

The aids for leg-yielding are extremely beneficial for the co-ordination and feel of the rider. While pushing the horse away from the straight line with the inside leg on the girth, the inside rein asks for a little flexion to the inside while the outside rein directs the horse as to where he has to go, prevents too much neck bend and stops the horse from falling onto the outside shoulder. The outside leg can be used on the girth if the horse is trying to fall onto the shoulder, or a little further back if the quarters get too much in advance of the shoulders. Any of these possibilities can occur as the young horse learns to go sideways and an adjustment may have to be made every few strides. The horse must be kept going forwards and not allowed to move sideways too acutely at this stage. Having mastered these types of lateral movements, shoulder-in will be much easier to accomplish.

Evenness in the rein

If adequate time has not been spent on ensuring the horse is even in the rein and works in a round outline, he will not develop the correct muscles equally on both sides and is likely to take unlevel steps on turns and circles throughout Novice level work. This problem will manifest itself to a greater degree in Advanced work, in as much as the hind steps in extended and medium trot will not be of equal length. Flying changes will not be of equal length because, on the side that the horse does not work through, but blocks on the rein, the step will be shorter, while in trot half-pass the horse may well rock onto the shoulder on the side on which the rein is

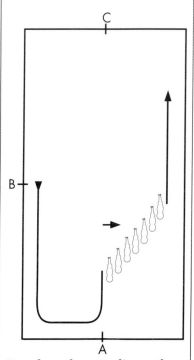

Turn down the centre line on the left rein, and leg-yield to the right.

Leg-yielding to the right, showing increased bend and angle.

too strong. Finally, the piaffe and passage steps will be irregular. To avoid running into these difficulties later on in the training, it is most essential to produce a novice horse that is even in the rein.

Bending and circling

On circles, the horse's spine, from his head to his tail, must look as if it is following the line of the circle and the outside hind leg must follow the path of the outside foreleg. When asked to trot or canter with more activity, some horses will place the inside hind leg on a line that is under the centre of the body. This often happens when the horse is weak or stiff and does not necessarily mean that the horse is crooked.

When viewed from the front on a circle, an imaginary line drawn down from the horse's nose should pass between his knees. The novice horse has to perform 20-m (66-ft) circles and 15-m (50-ft) and 10-m (33-ft) half-circles. He also has to cope with 90-degree corners and turns. Each corner and turn should be considered a quarter of circle and ridden to the capability of the horse. For example, when turning a young horse onto the centre line from the quarter marker on the long side, it is better to think of riding half a 10-m (33-ft) circle until the horse has started to bend round the rider's inside leg, after which the same track can be ridden as two corners.

Bending the horse prevents his muscles from stiffening and therefore enables him to use all the joints in his body with maximum efficiency.

The bending process starts with a lateral flexion that is asked for with the inside hand taking a little more weight on

A young horse leg-yielding to the left and looking loose, supple and attentive. The body is straight with a slight flexion to the right as the steps make ground forwards and sideways to the left.

Leg-yielding with a greatly increased bend. The horse is being pushed on to his left shoulder and into the left rein.

91

the rein, as if squeezing a sponge. The arm must not get tense in the process. A horse with a soft jaw should incline his head from the poll to the direction indicated so that the rider can see his eyelashes on that side. The outside rein must be given an adequate amount to allow for this to happen but an allowing connection must still be maintained. If the horse offers a bend in the neck – which he may do on his soft side instead of the correct flexion – the outside rein must prevent this and the horse should be straightened up and the flexion asked for again. If the leg pressure is not adequately maintained and adjusted when teaching the horse to bend, he will move his body into a position where he does not have to comply with the request. For example, if the right rein asks for a flexion, and the right leg is not pressing on the girth, the horse will step to the right. If the left leg is not slightly behind the girth, the quarters will step to the left. The stick should be used if the horse does not listen to the leg.

The next step to accomplish is a direction to the right and left. This is where the head and neck are positioned so that the imaginary line drawn down from the nose to the ground passes to the inside of the knee but the neck is straight from the withers to the poll. When the horse has got used to this, the shoulders can be placed fractionally to the inside, together with the head and neck. This position is called shoulder-fore. Basically, it prepares the horse for shoulder-in without expecting any bend and it helps to bring the shoulders away from the wall. As the horse's hindquarters are wider than his shoulders, this is a necessary procedure if he is to be taught to work straight. It also helps considerably in controlling the shoulders. If the horse is used to this position, he will accept a correction for 'too much bend' in the neck, which can develop in the more advanced work later on.

The trainer is aiming to have the horse uniformly bent round their inside leg, which means that the whole of the outside of the horse's body has to stretch. It is much easier to persuade the muscles in the neck to stretch than those over the rib cage, hence the problem of 'too much bend in the neck' can occur, which must be correctable. If the young horse is continually bent in the neck, the shoulders will fall to the outside and become very difficult to control, so that straightening the body will develop into a problem. Bending in the neck develops from the rider controlling excessively with the inside rein instead of aiming to have the horse 'between the inside leg and the outside rein'. (This is a term that is often used and has many computations. It will be discussed in

This horse is straight in the body with his neck positioned to the inside.

depth later.) At Novice level, it is enough to say that when the inside rein is released, the horse must stay on the line or circle and the neck should not deviate to the outside but remain in line with the shoulders, with the horse taking the outside rein forward. He must be straight on a straight line, curved on 20- or 10-m (66- or 33-ft) circles and in leg-yield or position right or left, remain round in outline and continue to work forward with the desired amount of impulsion when the inside rein is given. He is then said to be 'on the aids' and the rider can be satisfied that training is progressing well.

When circling and turning the young horse, the inside rein directs the horse along the desired track and asks for the flexion. The outside rein prevents too much bend in the neck. The combined effect of both reins keeps the horse's neck on the chosen line. The inside leg is used on the girth to keep the forward movement and to stop the body falling in. The outside leg is behind the girth to the extent that it prevents the quarters falling out but it should not push them to the inside, and the rider's weight is down into the inside stirrup through a lowered heel and a knee that drops as low as possible down the saddle flap to achieve this.

To arrive at this desired state of control, the horse must learn to accept and respond to the outside leg behind the girth. When first circling a newly broken-in horse, both legs rest quietly on the girth while riding the horse forward and trying to keep the shoulders on the desired line. As soon as possible, the horse should be taught to respond to the outside leg in as much as he moves his quarters to the side away from pressure behind the girth. The simplest way of beginning this response is to ask for a few steps of travers in walk. At this stage you will probably have just a straight horse in travers position. However, this does not matter as the main function of the exercise is to have the horse listening to the outside leg. When the horse has learnt to respond to the leg in this position, the rider will be able to prevent his quarters from swinging out. This will take some time to achieve in trot and canter circles but it must be possible before you can progress to competition at Novice level.

It can take quite a few months for an unbalanced young horse to execute a good 10-m (33-ft) circle and he should not be asked to do so until he is ready. A useful way of assessing his ability to make his circles smaller is to spiral in from a 20-m (66-ft) circle and, when the rider feels they have diminished the circle to the horse's ability, they can then push the horse out again from the inside leg, keeping the outside rein to prevent the shoulders running away from the inside leg and gradually developing a slight bend through the body round the inside leg. As with most exercises, this will be easier to do on one rein than the other and the experienced trainer will become used to finding that different problems occur to the right and to the left with each and every exercise that is taught to the horse. The final aim is to be able to control the horse so effectively that the dressage judge is unable to tell which is the horse's stiff side!

Working in circles is essential to the development of the trot and canter. The smaller the circle, the more the inside hind leg has to be used. The inside hind leg on the stiff side of the horse will not bend or step underneath the body as easily as that on the soft side and the horse will try to avoid using it by swinging the quarters out on the stiff side, falling out through the shoulder and bringing the quarters in on his soft side.

The untrained horse is inclined to lean in on a circle but the more advanced he becomes, the more upright he will become. The rider's body must always be at the same angle as the horse, neither leaning in more nor slipping to the out-side.

As the horse becomes proficient on a large circle, he can be worked in more demanding movements, i.e. serpentines, figures of eight, half-circle and back to the track. As he changes direction, he must keep the same rhythm. If he loses his balance, the rhythm will alter and become faster. When this happens, the rider must slow the speed and let the horse regain his balance and rhythm before riding forward again. This control of the speed is essential to the improvement of the balance. If you put impulsion into an unbalanced horse, you exacerbate the problem and push him further onto his forehand. Therefore, to rebalance a horse, you must slow down the speed, re-establish the rhythm and outline, if nec-essary, and then ride him forward with as much impulsion as he can manage. As the horse's training progresses, you must keep the feeling of riding him forward and containing the impulsion as you slow him down. In the beginning, the horse will not be able to manage this and the sensitive rider will monitor the amount of impulsion that they create so that it does not disturb the rhythm and the balance of the horse, nor cause excessive tension.

The trot must always be purposeful but there will be prob-lems if the rider creates more impulsion than the horse can handle. The rider must feel what the hind legs are doing, especially round corners and on circles. As the trot becomes more active and supple, so the horse will use his body and his joints should begin to work more efficiently, in which case the hind feet will not be left on the ground for so long and will work through under the body. The action of all the joints in the hind legs should be equal. If one is excessive, there is a probability that another is not working correctly. For exam-ple, a sharp snatchy action in the hock can mean that the stifle or fetlock joint is not working fluently.

Developing the working canter

At this stage of training it is usual for the trot to develop more rapidly than the canter. It is easier to straighten the trot, to control the shoulders in trot and slow down the trot. Most new exercises are taught and executed in trot before being done in canter.

A horse with a big, springy canter, who covers at least his own length with each stride and feels as if he is negotiating a cavaletto as he does so, is not easy to control. However, we should be pleased if he canters in this way as it will then be easier to develop the trot into a purposeful springy and elegant gait and care must be taken to develop it without spoiling it.

The most usual way in which the rider affects the canter adversely is to force the horse to canter slowly before he is physically strong enough or balanced enough to do so. The reins are taken strongly in an attempt to restrain the pace, the horse shortens his neck, is not able to use his head and neck in the correct way as he bounds along and the normal three-time gait loses its springy moment of suspension and occasionally turns into a flat four-time gait as well.

The canter is described as a left or right canter, depending on the leading foreleg. The sequence of canter when the left foreleg leads is off hind, then near hind and off fore together, then the left fore (leading leg), followed by the moment of suspension. The four-time canter is produced by the diagonal pair of legs being split, normally by the hind leg coming down before the foreleg, caused by slowing the speed before the horse is ready to do so and also by lack of impulsion and the horse not working through the rein in a round outline.

Another problem the trainer experiences with a young horse is the disunited canter. This is when the hindquarters are cantering right while the left foreleg is leading. This is a distinct fault, due to loss of balance and stiffening in the body, especially when the rider sits to the outside, uncoordination from the horse caused by physical weakness, a lack of desire to go forward or an insensitive and unallowing rein contact from the rider. To correct this fault, the young horse must be brought back to trot, rebalanced and asked to canter again. The rider must make sure that the saddle is central on the horse's back and that their weight is well to the inside.

Cantering is the most difficult gait in which to straighten the horse and, therefore, from the start, it is worth taking care not to canter the horse with too much inside rein, as an excessive bend in the neck will make the shoulders very difficult to control. This problem often begins with the rider bringing the head excessively to the inside, to indicate to the horse to lead with the inside foreleg.

A well-balanced, attentive halt.

Top left: **Entering the arena, alert and full of confidence.**

Bottom left: **A good medium trot, clearly showing the moment of suspension.**

Below: **A Medium horse working with impulsion and perfect balance.**

The horse is beginning to stretch his topline and take the hand forward and down to loosen up, although he has not stretched down fully yet.

The same horse in later work, showing a balanced and elastic working trot.

Right: Extended trot. Here, the neck is short with the shoulder lowered. The front leg has flicked up and must be drawn back, with the heel lower than the toe, before reaching the ground.

Below: A horse taking long strides in trot without dropping his shoulder. The foot is lowered flat to the ground at the end of the step.

Above: Working canter. This horse is not sufficiently engaged behind and is carrying too much weight on his shoulders.

Left: Cantering freely forward without falling on to the forehand.

A well-proportioned young horse that has muscled up correctly through training. Note the rider's position – straight lines from the ear through shoulder and hip to heel, and from elbow through the hand to the horse's mouth.

Top right: Showing a lengthened stride out of working trot.

Bottom right: The same horse has now lost his balance and his weight is more on his forehand.

Below: Although at present a little flat and unbalanced, this young horse is showing an impressive length of stride.

Preparing shoulder-in left –
coming out of the corner;
developing a bend round the
inside leg; positioning the horse at
the correct angle.

Walking pirouette to the left, showing the horse maintaining a good bend round the rider's inside leg.

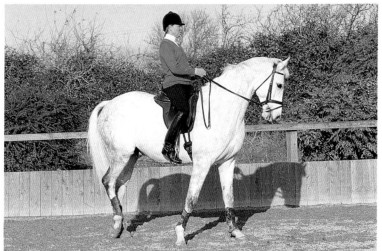

Top right: A horse nicely balanced in working canter and showing counter-canter with the off-fore leading.

Below: Starting to show collected trot.

Bottom right: Medium trot, showing good impulsion.

Top left: Half-pass right, showing a good bend.

Top right: Half-pass in left canter, showing the moment of suspension and a good springy gait.

Right: Half-pass in trot, showing a modest bend to the left.

The aids for canter

The aids for canter left are, first of all, to check the working trot for roundness, balance and impulsion. The rider should also check that their legs are in good contact with the horse's sides and that their weight is well down into the inside stirrup. With the young horse, it is helpful to work on a left-hand circle or to ask for the strike-off in the first corner going into the short end of the arena. The left leg, being the inside leg, is used close on the girth to keep the horse going forward. The inside rein asks for a position to the left, with a slight flexion at the poll, while the outside rein prevents an unwanted bend in the neck. The outside leg, in this case the right leg, strokes back to a position behind the girth to indicate the strike-off so that the near fore is the leading leg. If the horse strikes off with the outside leading leg, he should be brought back to trot, repositioned and asked again. As the horse's body is naturally curved to the leading leg, it is easier, initially, for the rider to improve the canter on a circle. However, when the horse is first asked to canter up the long side of the arena, most will have their hindquarters well to the inside of the line and it can be a considerable time before the rider has sufficient control of the shoulders to be able to canter straight down the long side of the school.

As the horse improves in his trot work, this improvement will be reflected in the canter and so repeated transitions from one to the other, on a circle, will benefit both gaits. The canter will add impulsion to the trot, while, in trotting, it is easier to rebalance and improve the outline if these have been lost in the canter.

Transitions and half-halts

Along with the half-halt, the correct execution of transitions has the biggest influence of all training techniques on the development of the horse's way of going.

At Novice level, all transitions may be executed in a progressive manner, that is to say, coming from working trot to halt, the horse is first asked to slow down the trot, then make a few steps in walk before coming to halt. This procedure is reversed when making upward transitions. The advanced horse, with his hind legs well engaged, is expected to halt directly from any gait if required to do so. To make the desired smooth and fluent transitions, the horse must accept the rider's hand and have sufficient suppleness and impulsion in the gait in which he is working. If the working trot is not good, the transition up into canter or down into walk will show a variety of problems. The most frequent of these are caused by simple disobedience. The horse must go correctly, without laziness, and be totally attentive to the rein and leg aids. If he is not working through the contact, he will resist in his jaw against the restraining rein, dip and hollow his back, use the muscles under his neck and raise his head off the bit, leaving his hind legs out behind him. It will not be easy to make an obedient transition in this stiff position and, therefore, he will ignore the aid for as long as possible. Until the young horse gains enough strength to bring his hind legs underneath his body, he will not be able to execute a half-halt but he will be able to make pleasant and obedient downward transitions if given enough time to adjust his speed according to his balance and co-ordination.

The horse must be executing simple transitions fluently and obediently before the half-halt can be used to any effect. However, when half-halts are established, they will, by design, improve the downward transitions if used as a preparation, as they are, in themselves, a refined transition.

The aids for half-halt

The aids for half-halt are to correct the position, making sure the lower leg is in good contact and able to create sufficient energy to activate the hind legs and to restrain the forward movement carefully, so that the horse shortens his steps as he obeys the demand to slow down but still thinks forward and stays active. The rider's seat must allow for the shorter steps and, as soon as a suspicion of this has been felt, the rein must allow the forward movement once more. If the horse has been lying on the hand or pulling against the rein, the contact, having first been lightened momentarily, should now be offered to him at the required weight. It is easier for the horse to adjust his weight onto his hind legs on a circle before he can manage this on a straight line and he must learn to respond to the forward aids from a predominantly inside leg as the rein allows him forward. As the horse shows he understands what is wanted, he must be rewarded for his efforts.

The half-halt is best thought of as a downward transition, used to rebalance, and later on collect, the horse. It can be, and at the beginning of the training, should be, executed in a slow and calm manner as often as necessary. Use trot to walk transitions repeatedly to make the horse think of slowing down the trot, then graduate to transitions from working trot to very slow trot. When the horse can decrease his speed over approximately six steps of trot and then move forward again to working trot speed, he has accomplished a half-halt. As this exercise progresses, the number of steps taken during the slowing-down phase will decrease and the moving-forward phase will increase in balance and activity, but only if ridden with feel for the quality of rein contact so that the horse does not set his jaw and stiffen through the back. If, for some reason, the horse has become very strong in the rein, the contact should be lightened for several steps during the riding forward phase, to make him realise that there is nothing to lean on. After this, a normal connection should be re-established.

As training progresses, the half-halts will become more refined and will be beneficial in bringing the horse's weight more onto the hindquarters and so lightening the forehand.

Lengthened strides

When the horse accepts the half-halt and benefits from its use, we can think about lengthened strides. When the young horse is asked to lengthen his stride in trot or canter, he must not be allowed to lose his rhythm and run, therefore, before the rider uses their legs to lengthen, the horse must be half-halted to engage the hindquarters and then again if he loses his balance during the lengthening. The rider must allow the horse to lengthen his frame to take the longer steps but must feel immediately if his weight falls onto his forehand and take the necessary action. At first it is easier to keep the balance on a 20-m circle, by asking the horse to go forward in a stronger trot and then come back to working trot after a short while – say, half a circle. If this is repeated a few times, the horse will learn to balance himself while taking the longer steps. It is more difficult to bring the horse back to working canter from lengthening in canter than it is in trot, as it is alien to the horse's nature to canter slowly; left to his own devices, he would break into trot as a matter of course. Therefore, at first he will be unwilling to canter slowly, which creates a mental block, and, until he understands what is wanted, he will stiffen and resist. Added to this is the problem that, in canter, the weight is more likely to fall onto the outside shoulder and then the horse will be crooked and unable to slow down easily.

If the horse does not show an aptitude for lengthening his steps in trot, but merely increases his speed, two choices are open to the rider. One is to keep pushing the horse forward round the track on the outside of the arena, encouraging him to stay round and lengthening the neck, hoping that the steps will also lengthen. If a large field is available, this will be more stimulating for the horse to trot round, as long as the going is soft and preferably with another horse by his side to incite longer steps. If the horse prefers to canter instead of developing a stronger trot, he must be stopped and made to trot again.

The other method is to work on a circle and to half-halt and push forward alternately until the hind legs are sufficiently engaged to make the longer steps. The horse must be strong enough to do this. Another exercise is to use trotting poles on a circle and gradually work up to using a wider distance so that the steps become longer, as described in Chapter 3.

If the horse does not lengthen in canter, it is advisable to adopt a light seat, or even jumping position, and, keeping the horse extra round, or 'very deep', push him on until he covers the ground in the desired way, but again he must be allowed to lengthen his neck within the contact. Later on, when he can manage some counter-canter, a more desirable difference may be obtained when asking for some lengthening after cantering half a circle withe the outside lead.

Most young horses that have been specifically selected for a dressage career will readily lengthen their stride if correctly prepared. It is usually the horses that are being retrained, or prepared for eventing, that will present the trainer with a problem.

As the horse lengthens, the rider must feel whether he falls onto one or other of his shoulders. If the lengthening is asked for across the diagonal from a right-hand corner a very slight position to the right must be kept across the diagonal until arriving at the track, where the horse is straightened and then prepared in the position left for the immediate corner. Many horses will find it easier to lengthen in trot if the rider stays rising. As sitting trot is not obligatory in Novice tests, there is no rush to sit on the horse until his back is strong enough and he is happy to accept the rider in this way.

Sitting trot

To begin sitting trot on the young horse, you must first establish the best possible working trot (rising) and then sit for half a circle, making sure that you do not alter the feeling on the horse's mouth nor stiffen your back against the horse as you cease rising. The horse must not alter his rhythm as the rider sits and, to prevent this, it is best to sit for only a short distance and then rise again until the horse completely accepts the feel of the rider. If he hollows and alters his stride, bring him back to a slow, relaxed trot, with very little impulsion, until he gets used to the new feeling. Thoroughbred horses are more likely to object to sitting trot than warmbloods.

It must be remembered that, while working the horse in rising trot, it is essential to change the diagonal when changing the rein. I like to ride on the outside diagonal, i.e. to sit when the outside foreleg comes to the ground. This ensures that the horse muscles-up symmetrically.

Giving and retaking the rein

Another important exercise expected of the horse in a Novice test is to 'give and retake the rein'. This is an excellent way of testing the horse's balance and the quality of the rider's rein contact and it should be practised right through the horse's training from an early stage, not just prior to the Novice test. If the test asks for the rider to 'stroke the horse's neck' or give and retake the reins between two markers or over X, the rider is required to push both hands slowly forwards and then retake the contact in one continuous movement. A guideline for the distance covered during the give and retake is six steps of trot or canter, unless specified otherwise on the test sheet. The horse should stay in balance without increasing speed, or losing rhythm or outline. If the rider is asked to give the reins over a specified longer distance, the horse, without increasing speed, may stretch his neck forward and down, as though seeking the contact, until such time as the reins are picked up and the contact re-established.

To prepare the young horse for this exercise, one rein can be given away for a few steps while working on a circle and, on retaking it, you should release the other rein for a similar time. It is worth noting whether the horse's reaction is the same to each single rein (which, of course, it should be). It is possible, however, that he may hollow when only one side of his mouth is in contact with the rider, which signifies that the contact is faulty and must be corrected.

When the horse understands that he should stay in the same position while the contact on one side is released, both reins can be given as required in the test, usually in canter. As a training exercise, it is beneficial also to give the reins in trot.

When the horse is advanced and the reins can be given and taken again during medium trot or piaffe, the horse will then be in truly perfect balance.

Turning about the forehand

A further suppling exercise for the young horse, to check that he is obedient to the leg, is the turn on the forehand or the turn about the forehand, which I prefer. Having taught the horse to step forward and cross his legs over sideways in leg-yielding, to respond to the outside leg in a travers position and to control the shoulders to the inside in shoulder-fore, the turn on the forehand requires a much bigger step across, with the inside hind leg passing in front of the outside hind leg as the horse turns through 180 degrees.

The aids for turn on or about the forehand

To ask for a turn with the horse moving away from the rider's left leg, begin from a halt, keeping the horse well on the aids, or from a slow walk if this does not spoil the steps. Apply the left leg behind the girth and use the right leg on the girth to stop the shoulders falling to the right and to keep the horse thinking forwards. The reins prevent the horse from walking forward but allow the hindquarters to rotate round the fore-hand, with a slight flexion to the left. If a true turn on the forehand is wanted, the left foreleg is the pivot leg, which must move up and down minimally on the spot. As a train-ing aid, however, I prefer to allow the horse to move round taking very small steps forward with the forelegs, as it is then easier for him to cross over behind and this also keeps him thinking forwards. On no account must he be allowed to step backwards while doing this movement.

A more advanced version is for the horse to be bent in the same direction as that to which the quarters are moving, as in half-pass, in which case it is the outside leg that gives the nudges to make the horse step forward and across.

If the rider is able to control the bend, the shoulders and the steps, the turn can be made through 360 degrees. It is prefer-able to move forward on a straight line after the movement or if difficulties occur. The turn should be practised equally on both reins. When the horse is accustomed to responding to the leg aid in this way, he will also respond to the outside leg used behind the girth to prevent the quarters falling out on trot and canter circles.

Leg-yielding, shoulder-fore and turn on the forehand are

purely training exercises and not classical school movements. They are used solely as a means to an end.

Rein-back

The rein-back is a further obedience exercise that can be used to supple and engage the joints in the hindquarters. It should not be begun with a rider on the horse until a controlled halt, with the horse calmly accepting the closed leg and rein contact, has been established. However, I am in favour of teaching the young horse to step backwards in hand using a vocal command and pressure over the nose with the headcollar, as, if he objects to that, he is not likely to oblige with the weight of a rider on his back. If the young horse does not move back when in hand, a slight tap on the chest with the hand or a whip, in conjunction with the voice, will usually do the trick. It is obviously an asset if he knows what this command means in the stable and when being led to a field or opening gates, etc. When the time comes to teach the aids for rein-back in the arena, a person on the ground can again touch him on the chest as the rider gives the aids, which can be a help if the horse does not immediately comprehend what is wanted.

In rein-back the horse steps back by moving his legs in diagonal pairs, as in trot, but at the speed of walk and without a moment of suspension. If there is tension in the back or resistance in the mouth, the backward diagonal step can be split so that the movement is no longer in two-time. A definite four-time beat is an error, although if the feet are raised well and do not drag through the surface of the arena, and the hind feet stay on a straight line, an almost indistinct difference in the diagonal pairs is permissible. For perfection, however, they should move together.

The aids for rein-back

The aids for rein-back are to halt the horse square and to attention. The lower legs ask the horse to step back by sliding both legs simultaneously to a 'behind the girth' position, and at the same time the seat is lightened. A restraining hand prevents forward movement but allows the steps backwards, when they are offered, by giving a little, between each step. It is at this moment that the voice can be used to remind the horse what is wanted, as he has already been taught to respond in hand to the voice. By placing the legs behind the girth, it is easier to keep the backward steps straight. If the quarters deviate to one side, the leg on that side must be placed further back and pressed more strongly against the horse until he crookedness has been corrected.

A weak horse should not be asked for rein-back and a novice horse should only be asked for one or two steps at a time. If he rushes back, he should be halted after one step and patted, to curb any anxiety. If he resists, he should not be pulled back with the reins but reminded again in hand, with a schooling whip used on the chest. Any response to stepping back must be rewarded by a pat and cessation of the request, until the horse is familiar with the aids.

Problems at Novice level

The most usual problems apparent to judges at Novice level in the UK are that the outline in the working paces is not sufficiently round, and that the horse does not work sufficiently from behind through the rider's hand with controlled but lively impulsion. There is also often a problem with the contact so that the horse does not take the hand forward in a correct way. Young horses that continue to experience these difficulties will not develop mentally and physically in a manner that pushes their athletic ability to its utmost, and therefore will not fulfil their potential when trained on to a higher level.

CHAPTER 7

WORKING AT ELEMENTARY LEVEL

A horse that is ready to compete at Elementary level must be able to show improved working paces, resulting from an increased ability to handle roundness of outline and impulsion simultaneously, to a degree that the beginnings of collection are evident. The more difficult movements must be executed with the ease that signifies a stronger and more muscled horse that can balance himself effectively. Some Elementary tests include more collected movements than others, so a choice can be made according to the horse's progress. At this standard, the horse is also expected to perform medium trot and canter, 10-m (33-ft) circles and shoulder-in in collected trot, shoulder-in, extended trot, medium and extended walk, counter-canter, simple changes, 10-m (33-ft) circles in collected canter and a more precise rein-back as well as all the Novice movements.

Collection

It takes a long time before the horse is properly collected; the muscles that are needed for the degree of balance and impulsion will gradually develop as the horse is trained to Prix St George level.

At Elementary level, the horse is still being taught many new exercises that, when incorporated into the daily training session, will help to build up these muscles. However, the working paces must be good enough before these lateral exercises will improve the horse's way of going. It is possible to teach the horse the mechanics of shoulder-in, travers and half-pass, etc., but unless the quality in the gaits is maintained at the same time, the impulsion will be lost, the weight-bearing capacity of the hindquarters will not increase and the gaits may even deteriorate.

A horse is said to be collected when he moves with sufficient impulsion and suppleness to enable the joints in the hindquarters to bend and bear more of his body weight, thus lightening the previously heavier forehand. His head and neck are raised and arched from the poll, which is the highest point.

To obtain this desired state of training, the rider must understand fully the way to achieve it and also appreciate how long it will take. It is a process that cannot be hurried – short cuts will produce a horse whose appearance is not enhanced by his training and who is no longer a pleasure to ride.

The impulsion that the rider has been able to create and control at Novice and Elementary level is only a fraction of that which must be maintained when the horse reaches Advanced. However, even now this impulsion must still be contained and the horse taught that the leg not only means 'go forward' but also 'take higher and more energetic steps' by bending all the joints, while the rider contains some of the forward movement yet still asks the horse to be active. By degrees, the whole frame of the horse gradually shortens and grows taller and, ultimately, gives the impression of moving slightly uphill.

It is possible for the horse to shorten his neck and not his body. This is not desirable. What we must aim for is a compression of the whole horse so that it resembles a round, springy form with neither tension in the muscles nor anxiety of mind.

As the horse progresses daily into a more collected way of going, so he will become ready to accept the hand in walk to a greater degree. At Novice level, it has been sufficient to walk mostly on a long rein or to feel the horse's mouth very quietly without making any demands to shorten the steps for fear of disturbing the correct rhythm and sequence. Gradually, the speed of walk can be varied, bearing in mind that, ultimately, an extended, medium, and collected walk have to be shown. If the walk on a long rein has been cultivated so that the horse marches forward, covering as much ground as possible with long energetic steps, taking up the rein and still allowing the head and neck to stretch out within the contact would constitute an extended walk in an Elementary and Medium test.

The medium walk must still be unconstrained, with energetic steps that overtrack, but the horse must not be quite so long in the body as in extended walk. The horse must appear comfortable with the rider's contact, without his nose coming onto a line behind the vertical or any hollowing in his outline.

When starting to think of collected walk, it is important not to hold the horse at a slower speed. The steps should cover less ground but they must not be any less active. Now the head should be only just in front of the vertical, on a higher, arched neck, with each step being shorter and higher off the ground. If the horse is not in self-carriage, the rein will be too heavy and the sequence of steps will lose their rhythm and energy.

Initially, it is impossible to say to the horse in any gait 'please take short steps'. The rider has to experiment slightly with each horse to find the right amount of impulsion, relaxation, position and speed at which the horse learns for himself that a shorter step is the easiest way of going under those particular circumstances. When this has been worked out and the partnership on both sides knows what to do, the shorter step is activated to increase collection.

This is especially difficult in the walk where the steps are vulnerable to unlevelness if the rider tries to shorten them by too much restraining action on the rein. Whatever the speed of the walk, it is essential to keep the lower leg firmly in place and to follow the natural nodding movement of the head and neck with the hands. In collected walk there is much less nodding than in medium and extended walk, although there is still some movement. It is better to make walk to halt transitions frequently until the speed of the collected walk is established and then walk on 10-m circles before allowing the horse to stride out again on a straight line. When practising a slower, more collected walk, it is as well to have somebody watching to let you know if the steps remain even, positive and correct.

Working on the walk should be a daily exercise, as should be giving the horse a long rein. When the contact is picked up again, the horse must accept it and be round in outline. It is beneficial to teach the horse the aids for new movements in walk as there is more time for him to assimilate what is wanted without losing his balance or having to cope with the extra impulsion of trot at the same time.

Walk pirouette

The walk pirouette is a movement that activates the hind legs and therefore helps to produce collection. If used within the walk itself, it will produce shorter and higher steps and will also improve the trot and canter when the rider is able to make a transition to walk, immediately ask for a walk pirouette and then move off into the desired gait with activated hind legs.

The pirouette is at first a half-circle and later a full circle, in which the forehand moves round the hindquarters. Initially, the horse should be taught to move forward and sideways in walk, as it is imperative that the sequence of walk steps is maintained. When the horse becomes familiar with the aids, the turn should be executed within the length of the horse. The pirouette is not necessary the horse has to compete at Medium level so do not be in a hurry to achieve it. The horse should be bent round the rider's inside leg towards the direction of the shoulder movement. It is a far more difficult movement for the horse to execute than a turn about the forehand but it is necessary to teach the horse to move away from the leg, as in the turn on the forehand, before you can stop him moving into the leg and hold the hindquarters as required in half-pirouettes.

The aids for walk pirouette

The aids are as follows: the inside rein asks for a direction to the inside with a very slight bend round the inside leg. This is used to activate the inside hind leg which is not allowed to pivot but is moved up and down on as small a circle as the rider feels is right for the horse's level of training. The outside leg is place behind the girth to prevent the quarters swinging out but not to the extent that the horse moves his quarters too much to the inside as in half-pass – that would be wrong as the shoulders have to move round the haunches while the hind steps move up and down on the turn without actually crossing over. The rider's weight and seat should be well to the inside and both hands should be moved slightly towards the way the horse is bending so that the outside rein not only prevents too much bend in the neck but, by pressing against the neck, indicates to the horse to move the forehand round. (The hand is never carried over the withers, only very close to them.) As soon as the horse has taken the required amount of steps round, the outside leg should be placed on the girth and the horse ridden forward from the inside leg onto a straight line.

To start the walk pirouette ride the horse on a square of about 15 m (50 ft). At each corner make a 90-degree turn, involving two steps of walk pirouette. This is good preparation

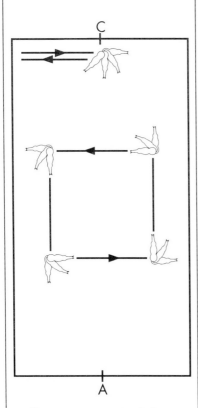

Walking a square to teach the horse to think forward while moving his shoulders round 90 degrees in preparation for walk pirouette. (A half-pirouette is shown by C.)

to the 180-degree turn and keeps forward movement upper-most in the mind of both horse and rider.

As the horse comes to terms with the various exercises in walk, so his aptitude to perform with more collection in the trot exercises will improve. In the Elementary standard tests all trot work has to be executed sitting but the horse should be given plenty of time to relax and loosen up in rising trot, which can include many of the preliminary exercises already mentioned in Chapter 6.

Shoulder-in

The most important and useful exercise in training the dres-sage horse is shoulder-in. This should only be begun when the working trot has sufficient balance and impulsion and the horse is strong and supple enough to benefit from bending round the rider's inside leg. If, once he understands the aids, the horse stiffens, hollows or loses impulsion when asked to perform shoulder-in, then he has not been properly prepared, or is not ready. He will gain no benefit from the exercise under these conditions; in fact, he will probably stiffen against the rider's inside leg.

The aids for shoulder-in

If shoulder-in is performed in the right way, the rider will have total control of the horse's shoulders and will be able to place him on three or four tracks along the wall or to right or left of the centre line. The horse should be marginally bent round the rider's inside leg and should be able to maintain impulsion and position on a 10-m (33-ft) circle as a prepara-tion for shoulder-in. The inside rein asks for the bend, while the outside rein controls it. The outside rein also prevents the horse from continuing on the line of the preparatory circle but, along with the inside leg on the girth, indicates that the horse must travel away from the direction in which he is look-ing, in this case up the track. The rider must move his or her weight to the inside by moving the seat to the inside, with the inside leg remaining long in order to remain effective. The outside leg is behind the girth to prevent the quarters swing-ing out, and therefore maintains the bend round the inside leg. Beginning shoulder-in on the track along the wall of the school will also prevent the quarters swinging out, however, and so it is not until it is performed down the centre line that you will find out how effective your outside leg is. Many Medium-level horses get into a shoulder-in position on the

Having turned on the centre line, the horse is being prepared for shoulder-in. The shoulders are slightly to the left, in shoulder-fore position.

centre line initially by moving their haunches out but this is not the correct start for the movement.

As the horse moves along the line he can be on either three or four tracks. The inside hind leg is placed in front of the outside hind leg, which is, technically, the manoeuvre that improves the use of the joints in the haunches, and the inside foreleg crosses in front of the outside leg.

Shoulder-in is used in all tests from Elementary standard to Intermediare 1. At the higher levels, it is performed in a more collected state. It is also used as a preparation for all lateral work in trot and canter and before walk and canter pirouettes. A good rider will be thinking 'shoulder-in right' or 'shoulder-in left' most of the time they are in the saddle, as this will help to maintain the control that is necessary to ride through a dressage test. When teaching the horse shoulder-in initially it is easier for him to learn the movement in walk. As soon as possible, however, he should progress to doing it in trot. The angle asked for should be very slight at first and only a few steps should be performed to start with.

Two main problems occur when introducing the horse to this movement. First, on the soft side, he finds it very easy to bend only the neck, which will make it difficult to bring the shoulders to the inside. The outside rein must be kept to prevent excessive neck bend, while the inside rein turns the horse in to the required position. With this problem it is better to straighten out the horse onto the track after having accomplished a few strides. This can be done two or three times down the long side of an arena. Second, on the stiff side of the horse it will be difficult to obtain a bend and it is advisable to make the bend in the neck coming out of a corner or small circle before bending the body round the inside leg, as it is possible to get a position without any bend at all, which is leg-yielding, and the stiff horse will try to adopt this position instead of the more difficult shoulder-in. After a few steps, instead of straightening onto the track, move forward onto a circle, as this will help to keep the horse supple for the exercise.

The rider should be flexible as to how to finish the first few steps of shoulder-in. The above suggestions can be reversed, depending on how the horse reacts to the exercise. If the horse finds the bend easy and the angle difficult, it may be more advantageous to finish by turning the shoulders off the track, or circling, to get them used to moving away from the boards. If the horse is very stiff and the angle is too much without any bend, the shoulders must be taken back to the

Left: **Shoulder-in established on three tracks, with the horse making active steps and in good balance.**

track to reduce the angle and then the rider should ask for the necessary bend in the neck before repositioning the shoulders.

A useful exercise to help to put the horse into shoulder-in is to turn down the centre line on the left rein, leg yield to the right to the outside track (in a long arena this would be to approximately half-way). On reaching the track, bend the horse round the left leg, which has been used to produce the leg-yielding, and ride on down the track in shoulder-in position. It can be easier to produce the movement this way rather than asking from a corner or circle. As with all new exercises, the rider will discover the best place to get a response from the horse and this will vary according to the ability of each individual. When the horse is correctly bent round the rider's inside leg, it should be possible to give away the inside rein for a few strides without any alteration in the progression of the movement. This is another proof of the horse being completely between the inside leg and the outside rein.

When shoulder-in is established, the circles and corners will become easier to ride. It is not possible to ride a proper corner, i.e. one quarter of a 6-m (20-ft) circle – a volte – until the horse can perform shoulder-in. If you cannot correct the horse in the corners and keep him in balance, you will not be able to correct him in half-pass or other advanced movements. In a volte the horse has the same bend as in shoulder-in but at this standard you should adjust the size of the circle to match the horse's capabilities. He must be able to go well into a corner before managing a 6-m (20-ft) circle. If riding shoulder-in down the long side, always straighten out and ride into the corner on a single line to test your control and to teach the horse how to work in the corners, thus preparing him for test riding.

Straightening the horse in canter

The canter is a an asymmetric gait and therefore one in which the horse is naturally more likely to be crooked rather than straight.

The same shoulder-in aids that are used to position the horse for this exercise in trot are also used to straighten the horse in canter, as it is the shoulder that falls off the desired line to the outside, causing the horse to be crooked. This gives the appearance of the quarters coming to the inside and the forehand going to the outside along the track on which the horse is travelling. However, when giving the aids in canter to

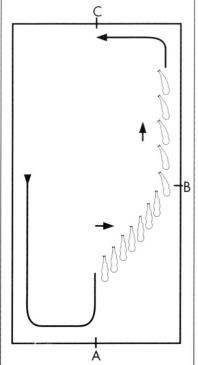

Above: **Leg-yielding from the centre line towards B, gradually developing a bend into shoulder-in down the track.**

The horse is now demonstrating
shoulder-in on four tracks.

Shoulder-in, clearly showing the
horse to be on four tracks.

bring the shoulders more to the inside, it is not necessary nor desirable to bend the neck. The same aids are applied but the outside rein prevents the neck bend and the effect of the aids should be only to straighten the body or have the shoulders minimally to the inside and with less angle than is required in trot.

On a 20-m (66-ft) circle, a slight position of shoulder-in can be asked for in trot and canter to activate the inside hind leg and so increase collection. The inside hind leg is made more active in this position, as the horse is bent round the rider's inside leg and therefore this leg has to step further under the body in this situation. As long as the horse stays correct in the hand and is free from resistance, the joints should bend in the way that is required for collection. However, this is a difficult position to maintain because the horse will prefer to place his haunches to the outside to avoid the increased engagement. Alternating shoulder-in with a few steps of travers should help to solve the problem of the

Above left: Shoulder-in with the horse on three tracks

Above right: Shoulder-in on three tracks with more bend in the neck than through the body.

Left: Shoulder-in showing too much angle and lack of engagement, thus causing the nose to come behind the vertical.

quarters deviating to an undesirable position, as the horse will be reminded to listen to the outside leg and the rider can then keep the haunches on the line of the circle.

Travers

In travers, the horse is again bent round the inside leg of the rider to the same angle as in shoulder-in. The main differences in the two movements are that, in travers, the horse moves in the direction in which he is looking and the neck is slightly straighter than in shoulder-in, the bend in the body materializing from the big crossing-over steps performed by the hind legs. When performing this exercise down the long side of the arena or down the centre line, the horse's forehand and chest stay straight on the line with the neck parallel to the wall. Because of this the young horse usually finds it more difficult to master and it is advisable to teach the movement in walk before trying it in trot. Later, it can be used in canter to engage the hind legs but it should not be used in this gait until the horse obeys the shoulder-in aids proficiently in canter, as travers in canter makes for a very crooked horse and so an equal distance in travers and shoulder-in should be worked on alternately. Never allow the horse to use travers as an evasion from being straight. Because of this risk, it is unwise to perform travers in canter down the long side of the arena as, normally, the rider is trying to prevent the horse adopting this position of his own accord. Travers in canter is better done on a large circle to engage the hind legs or down the three-quarter line to test the rider's control and prepare for half-pass.

The aids for travers

The aids for travers to the left are as follows: the rider's weight must be to the inside, with the left leg pressing in by the girth for the horse to bend round. The right leg is placed behind the girth to ask the quarters to step to the left. The left rein keeps the horse's neck on the line and asks for a slight flexion. The tendency at this stage is for the horse to want to place his head and neck to the outside and so adopt a leg-yielding position in order to avoid bending round the inside leg. The outside rein helps to regulate the speed if the horse tries to run away from the leg but it cannot be used much, otherwise the horse would adopt the wrong bend.

When teaching the horse the movement in walk, it is helpful to make an 8-m or 10-m (26- or 33-ft) circle somewhere

along the long side of the arena. A few strides before getting back to the track, apply the travers aids in order to ask the horse to step to the inside before reaching the track where he expects to be allowed to go straight. It is more difficult to move the quarters off the track to achieve the same position. If the horse objects to the travers movement, it will help to remind him what is wanted by asking for a turn about the forehand with a flexion to the direction in which the quarters are moving. Having been taught a few steps of travers along with the turn about the forehand, it should not be difficult for the horse to execute travers up the long side of the arena, first in walk and very soon in trot.

Travers is a forerunner of half-pass but it is essential to be

133

able to execute it smoothly, without loss of balance, rhythm, impulsion or flexibility, before attempting half-pass. If any of these problems are evident in travers, they will manifest themselves in the half-pass position and it will be a more difficult to correct the horse along the line of half-pass, although the aids for the two movements are the same.

The improved engagement in the trot, that is achieved from working in shoulder-in, should have begun to make it easier to slow down the speed in canter. A lot of time should be spent on pushing the horse forward and bringing him back in both trot and canter. At first, ask for a stronger working pace in trot or canter on a 20-m (66-ft) circle. As soon as the horse feels as if his weight is going onto his forehand, he must

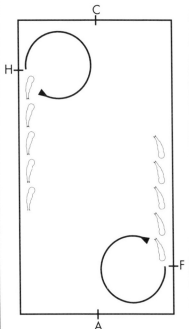

Above: Shoulder-in from a 10-m (33-ft) circle at F and travers from a 10-m circle at H.

Left: More angle in travers, with the horse now on four tracks.

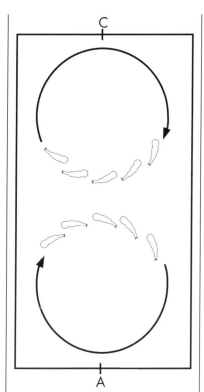

Above: **Shoulder-in on a 20-m (66-ft) circle at A and travers on a 20-m circle at C.**

be brought back to a slower working speed. Gradually, both ends of the speed scale can be increased so that the medium paces are developed. These are between the working and extended paces and, although the horse might be able to manage the longer, active steps, because of the added impulsion, it is the ability to slow down again without losing the outline and rhythm and to stay softly on the bit that may cause problems. The more he is brought back to being 'extra slow', as in half-halting, for a few steps from a working speed, the quicker he will realize what is wanted and come back from the stronger pace.

Canter to walk transitions – simple changes

It is necessary to be able to slow the canter down sufficiently before asking for a canter to walk transition. At Elementary standard this downward transition may be progressive, but, even allowing for a few steps of trot before walking, the speed of the canter must be towards collection. Cantering on a 10-m (33-ft) circle greatly improves the engagement of the inside hind leg and gives the horse the idea of a slower speed. When first asking for canter to walk, establish obedience and understanding on a 10-m (33-ft) circle before asking on a straight line such as the diagonal, as the horse's weight will be more underneath him on the curve of a circle. Initially, do not ask for the upward transition too soon but really establish a good medium walk (and, ultimately, a collected walk) before departing into trot and then canter again. When working on these more advanced transitions, it is a mistake to try to ride them as required in the test straightaway. Aim at everything being very progressive and sure, slowly building up to making a correct simple change; i.e. canter slowly, two or three steps in trot, two or there steps of walk and then into canter again with the new leading leg.

The Elementary tests also require a change of canter lead through trot. This is not a simple change but is a very good exercise for preparing the horse for it. When practising these transitions, do not always change the lead but keep the horse attending to your leg aids by 'out of sequence strike-offs'.

Walk to canter is not a difficult exercise for a horse. They do it out in the field every day. It is the question of being obedient to the aid and staying in the correct outline that causes difficulties. To start with, the easiest place to ask for walk to canter is in a corner, as the horse will be used to going into canter from trot in this place. Then it can be attempted across the centre line as if on a serpentine or figure of eight and, lastly, on the centre line where it will be difficult to keep the horse straight and a few steps of position towards the leading leg must be achieved in walk prior to cantering.

If the horse starts anticipating any of the above transitions, drops behind the bit or tries to hollow in his outline, revert to riding forward and making alterations to the speed within the gaits, keeping him well in front of your leg. Once they have learned how to do it, horses will often try to canter slowly instead of working forward properly in trot. This usually happens when they are not straight and any tendency to do this must be corrected immediately. The slower canter can sometimes become a four-time beat or, more usually, will lose the moment of suspension if maintained for too long without sufficient energy from the hind legs. Again, this is cured by pushing the horse forward towards a medium canter and then bringing him back with the feeling that you are still riding him forwards, trying to maintain the spring that creates the moment of suspension.

It is helpful to have somebody watching from the ground when altering the speed of canter, until the rider is sure that the slower canter is keeping the correct sequence of steps and energy. Also, unless a mirror is available in which to watch the canter on the centre line, a person standing at C is invaluable to say whether the canter, and the transitions in and out, are straight, and whether the corrections are sufficient or not. To straighten the canter on the centre line, it is necessary to make shoulder-fore or position to the right or left as described in Chapter 6.

Counter-canter

The horse must be familiar with being straightened in the canter before you ask him to perform counter-canter. Counter-canter is when the horse is asked to canter on a line with the outside foreleg leading as opposed to the inside foreleg. This line can be in the shape of a shallow loop, a half-circle and back to the track, with the steps of canter on down the track becoming the outside lead, round the short end of the arena, or on a circle. Counter-canter is an extremely unbalancing movement if the horse is still on his forehand and without sufficient engagement of the hind legs. The rider must not keep the counter-canter by asking for an excessive bend in the neck to the leading leg. This practice will make the horse very crooked as the shoulder will fall

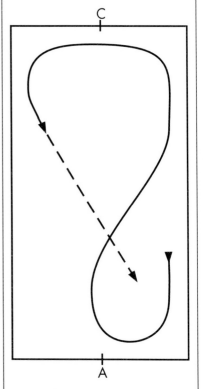

A more difficult counter-canter exercise. Half-circle back to the track and keep the outside lead round the short end. Ask the horse to lengthen his steps over the diagonal to help to engage the hindquarters correctly.

out, i.e. away from the leading leg, and so detract from the quality of the canter. The horse must be kept in the desired canter lead by riding in the shoulder-fore position to the leading leg, hence making the horse accustomed to this procedure on a straight line first.

When the horse is sufficiently balanced to perform counter-canter without hollowing, losing rhythm, increasing speed, changing both legs or cantering disunited, the exercise is an important contribution to increased engagement of the hindquarters and will encourage the horse to use his back and therefore help towards developing collection. These improvements will also be evident in the trot work. After doing some counter-canter exercises, the horse will trot with increased energy and body movement showing that he has benefited from the suppling and engagement that this movement encourages.

The shallow loop is the easiest line on which to perform counter-canter and the loop can be made deeper as the horse's proficiency increases. When first going round a corner, always make a large curve and cut the corner to avoid the risk of unbalancing the horse. The route can be made more difficult as the horse becomes more accomplished, until he can manage the whole of the short end of the arena, serpentines of three loops in a 20 x 60-m (66 x 198-ft) arena and then a figure of eight in a 20 x 40-m (66 x 130-ft) arena, part of which has to be shown in the Elementary tests.

The horse should not be allowed to break into trot from counter-canter of his own accord. If he does, the canter must be re-established on the same lead immediately and the horse must only be brought back to trot when the rider thinks it best. If, after or during the counter-canter, the horse feels very crooked, some straightening of the canter on the centre line will be beneficial.

Problems at Elementary level

The most usual problem that a judge of Elementary classes will see is a lack of weight-bearing capacity and engagement from behind. As already mentioned, the degree of collection is an ongoing process throughout the training, apparent to the rider, trainer and judge as the horse's physique develops. At Elementary level, the collection is only expected to be indicated, giving the judge an impression of correct balance and activity so that more collection from that particular horse can easily be imagined. The steps in collected trot can be the same

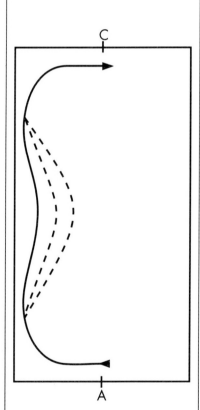

A shallow loop used when introducing the horse to counter-canter. Gradually make the loops deeper.

length as those in working trot as long as they are a little higher, with more bend in the joints, and maintain the same rhythm. The judge does not want to see a slower speed with shorter steps and less impulsion.

The medium trot and canter, and later the extensions, will improve as collection develops. The judge does not want to see the steps lengthening in front only and not from behind. Both front and back steps should lengthen with obvious impulsion. The nose can be slightly more in front of the vertical than in working and collected trot and the head and neck a little lower and longer without losing balance.

All this is achieved by perfecting half-halts in conjunction with keeping the horse in front of the leg. The Novice half-halts were conducted slowly, giving the horse time to decrease speed and get used to the restraining control before releasing the rein and asking him to go forward again. The timing with the Elementary horse, bordering on collection, is a little more vital. By that I mean that the restraining rein aid, to contain the created impulsion, and the allowing of the rein should be quicker than before. The exercise should be done with less delay and be repeated far more often, if necessary, to achieve the desired result. Depending on their natural balance and ability, horses vary as to how much the half-halt has to be used. Many horses need to be prepared with a half-halt before certain movements if they do not feel well balanced. The half-halt should also be used to help to store up energy for medium and extended gaits.

The extended gaits will eventually cover the maximum amount of ground with each step as a result of the stored-up energy, that has been created in the collection, being released and the rider must allow the horse to lengthen his neck and his body in order to do this without leaning on the rein or losing his balance. As with collection, extensions in Elementary tests are only the beginnings and it is very difficult for a horse to manage the required balance and impulsion on a line across the diagonal in a 20 x 40-m (66 x 130-ft) arena. A 20 x 60-m (66 x 198-ft) arena gives the horse and rider more time to make the transitions into and out of extension without feeling cramped and short of space.

It is worth remembering that it is possible to have collection without being able to extend properly but it is not possible to extend well without the engagement of the hocks and lightness of the forehand necessary for collection. Therefore, if the horse's extensions are disappointing, work on

developing the collected gaits and this will also improve the extension.

The rein-back steps must now be counted. Usually four are asked for but it is not wise to practice only four steps of rein-back. Vary the amount daily and be able to move forward in walk or trot after either one, or up to five, steps. Together with the rein-back, it is important also to practise the immobility, as from now on this will have to be shown in the tests. The horse must remain on the bit, standing square and motionless for a few seconds before either reining-back or departing into walk or trot. When he reaches Advanced level, he must also go forward to canter from rein-back or into passage.

The horse in rein-back, with the rider adopting a light seat and the lower leg behind the girth. The steps are of sufficient length, although the head and neck are a little high and short.

139

If the rein-back steps become lazy, with the horse dragging his feet through the surface of the arena, you can help to energize the steps by halting directly from trot and then immediately stepping back. As both rein-back and trot are diagonal steps, the one can help the other.

At this point it is necessary to make the horse halt square by using a leg on the girth on the side on which the hind leg has been left behind, until, eventually, the horse will bring the hind legs up square of his own accord. 'Halt not square' is a reflection of the balance of the movement from which the horse has been halted, so think of curing the cause and not the symptom, remembering to half-halt before halting.

An Elementary test may be ridden in a snaffle or double bridle. If the horse is of tender years and is going well enough to be placed at Elementary level, there is no need to ride in a double bridle. If there are any problems at this stage, they should be put right while still wearing a snaffle bridle. The use of the double bridle should come at a later stage rather than earlier in the training and its aim should be to refine a totally correct feeling in the rein and a correct way of going (see page 162).

CHAPTER 8

WORKING AT MEDIUM LEVEL

A horse that is ready to compete at Medium level must have the ability to show work from collection through to extension, while staying round, supple and in balance. The transitions may no longer be progressive and the whole test should look accurate and precise with a marked impression that the horse is really developing in advanced self-carriage. All three gaits have to be shown in collected, medium and extended form

Lengthening the stride for medium canter.

CHAPTER 8

WORKING AT MEDIUM LEVEL

Lengthening the stride for medium canter.

A horse that is ready to compete at Medium level must have the ability to show work from collection through to extension, while staying round, supple and in balance. The transitions may no longer be progressive and the whole test should look accurate and precise with a marked impression that the horse is really developing in advanced self-carriage. All three gaits have to be shown in collected, medium and extended form

141

and there is far greater emphasis on the transitions in and out of these progressions.

The horse must also show shoulder-in, travers and half-pass in trot and half-pass in canter, as well as a more difficult form of counter-canter than at the lower standard. From this level upwards, walk pirouettes are also included in the tests.

Collection should now be shown in its true form, although not yet with as much power or cadence as is required for the Advanced FEI tests (Fédération Equestre International is the governing body through which all international competitions are run and whose rules are accepted by competitors in the UK and other countries.) However, a sufficiently lightened forehand and engaged hindquarters enhance his natural paces and outline so that the movements look easy and the horse appears a pleasure to ride.

The greatest problem the trainer has at this stage is to increase the impulsion while staying in control and keeping the horse from becoming strong in the rein and yet still maintaining a correct outline. It is often the case that the neck shortens while the body remains a little to long with the hind steps not coming sufficiently under the body. When this happens, the nose is inclined to come behind the vertical, giving the appearance of a horse that is being held to the desired speed and that is not taking the rider's hand forward. This outline is not correct and will be marked down in competition.

There are three big hurdles to overcome when training the horse to Grand Prix. The first is obtaining sufficient and correct collection at Medium level; the second is teaching the horse flying changes; and the third is establishing piaffe and passage. I will go into more detail about the second and third later. At this stage it is worth remembering that the better the collection is established, the easier the training will be in the future.

Half-pass

The half-pass in trot will show up any lack of collection immediately. If the horse is not moving with sufficient self-carriage, impulsion and suppleness, it will be difficult to keep the bend, the balance and the engagement. The horse will appear stiff, fall onto his forehand and lose forward movement. The horse will often find it easier to make the half-pass in canter, as the body is more naturally bent in this gait. As the hind legs do not have to cross over, it is possible to perform

Half-pass to the left in trot, showing a good crossing over of the front legs.

canter half-pass in quite a strong working canter, which will often loosen the horse up well before asking for more collected work.

The aids for half-pass

The aids for half-pass from a right-hand turn or circle are as follows: keep the horse bent round the inside leg (the right leg) by putting him into position right with the inside rein so that he is looking at the marker to which you have planned to ride. The outside rein (the left rein) prevents too much bend in the neck. The rider also looks towards the point at the end of the diagonal line to which they are riding and puts their weight to the inside by pressing firmly into the stirrup and keeping the leg long and secure against the horse by the

143

girth, in order to give him something to bend around. When the horse is in the correct position, the outside leg (the left leg) is used behind the girth to ask him to cross the near fore and near hind in front of the off fore and off hind as he travels forwards and sideways on the chosen diagonal line.

A great deal of preparation is required in order to carry out a stylish half-pass. It is very easy for the horse to throw weight onto the inside shoulder as he moves across but if he does this he will lose any bend that has been established round the rider's inside leg. The rider must keep the inside leg securely on the girth and use it sufficiently to keep the horse bent round the leg as well as driving him forward.

Riding a few steps of shoulder-in prior to moving across in half-pass will position the horse satisfactorily. In fact, it is helpful to think about riding shoulder-in within the half-pass movement as a matter of course. As soon as the bend becomes insufficient, the remedy is to go into a few steps of shoulder-in before continuing with the half-pass once more.

Start by familiarizing the horse with the movement in walk and then, as soon as possible, progress to trot because the movement does not flow as easily in walk as it does in trot and canter.

It is important, initially, to keep the half-pass line going well forward as opposed to too much sideways and also not to be too ambitious with the amount that you ask for. For example, if turning up the centre line at A from a left-hand turn, having positioned the horse and moving into half-pass between the letters D and L, the most appropriate line for a young horse would be towards S or even H. The horse will always move more freely towards the track than away from it so bear this in mind when incorporating half-pass into the daily training routine. Later on, when the horse becomes more proficient, half-pass can be asked for from the track towards the centre line and, ultimately, all the way across the arena. As the collection develops, so the angle of the half-pass can be increased, but be careful not to ask for a difficult-angled half-pass until the collected trot warrants it and the suppleness of the horse allows it. A few good steps are far better than several moderate steps that become progressively worse.

Likely problems to be aware of when beginning to teach the horse half-pass are the difficulty of maintaining the bend round the inside leg and keeping the rhythm of the trot steps. If the horse becomes tense or stiff, the rhythm may become hurried and the speed increase. It is helpful to think of 'slow, big steps' as the horse progresses sideways, to prevent the

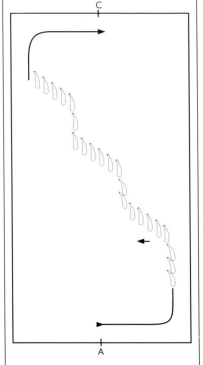

A helpful movement for the Medium horse is half-pass into shoulder-in, repeated several times over the diagonal.

Right: Half-pass to the right in trot but with insufficient bend.

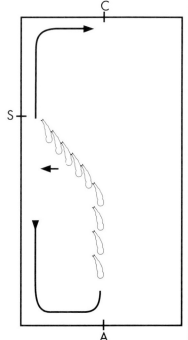

Above: Shoulder-in left up the centre line and half-pass towards S.

rhythm becoming hurried and to give the horse time to cross over in the desired manner. The horse must also stay round enough and not lose his balance and fall onto his forehand. This is why sufficient collection is imperative before starting half-pass. A half-halt can be made within the half-pass movement if a lack of balance and a strong rein warrant it. Lastly, the quarters must not be ahead of the shoulders when viewed from the front. This is known as 'quarters leading'. If this happens, use less outside leg and think more about shoulder-in position to bring the shoulder marginally ahead of the quarters.

If the half-pass finishes with a feeling of not going forward, push the horse into a stronger trot or medium trot when you have straightened him out. If he has become strong in the 145 hand and rather onward-bound because of the pressure of your legs, he must be half-halted, rebalanced and lightened in the rein; possibly, you should do some shoulder-in to re-establish the collection.

Straightening the horse

It is necessary to make a horse truly straight after moving sideways, especially if going up the centre line towards the judge at C. This can be a fairly difficult exercise. To straighten the horse after making half-pass to the right, it is essential to keep direction right to prevent the shoulder bulging to the left, and also to be able to ride forward from the inside leg. Decrease the bend by taking a more positive feel with the outside rein. Bring the outside leg more towards the girth position to stop the sideways steps but the legs must keep the horse positively on the centre line and moving forward.

When riding down the centre line to turn to the right or left at C, the rider must prevent the outside shoulder taking the whole horse in a bulging line off the track away from the turn. This is a rider error and it can be avoided by making sure the horse is positioned to the right or to the left and held securely between the inside leg and outside rein before the turn.

The same tactics are necessary when riding across the diagonal. For example, from a right-hand corner onto the diagonal line, a fraction of position right must be maintained until reaching the track one horse's length before the marker, straightening out, and riding the left-hand corner round the new inside leg, and vice versa.

The half-pass in canter is easier for the horse when the angle is small, which it should be at Medium level. However, the horse must not always be too free, and a more acute degree of angle will gradually encourage weight onto the hind legs and therefore increase collection and improve the canter.

If problems occur in the trot or canter half-pass, it is as well to revert to travers in both gaits, as the various problems will be easier to sort out in this movement. The horse should be really fluent in travers in various places in the arena, especially down the centre line where total control of the shoulders can be easily assessed, before attempting the more difficult movement of half-pass. Half-pass is travers along a more difficult route, i.e. a diagonal, the aids and the position of the horse in both movements being identical. The easier line is parallel to the long side, where the wall or side of the

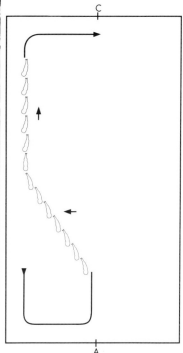

Left: Canter half-pass left, showing too much neck bend.

Above: Half-pass into renvers from trot or canter if the quarters have been trailing.

school helps to keep the shoulders on the desired track. If the quarters have been trailing in half-pass, it can help to finish before the track and position the horse in renvers. This is the same as travers but with the quarters towards the wall instead of the shoulders. Likewise, if the horse has finished half-pass with not enough bend, ride the horse forward into shoulder-in. Every horse has a different problem and most horses are dissimilar on each side, so that different tactics are required to the right and to the left. The skilled rider will react accordingly and make the necessary corrections.

It can be said that it is more difficult to straighten the horse after half-pass in canter than after half-pass in trot. The horse is naturally more bent to the leading leg in canter and the half-pass develops this bend. The freedom to open up the shoulder

147

Renvers in left canter, with the horse correctly bent round the rider's inside leg.

Renvers on the inside of the track, showing less bend and angle.

and take an impressive forward and sideways step is governed by the degree of bend in the neck. Too much bend in the neck in either gait will inhibit the freedom of the shoulders, therefore it is essential that the rider learns to feel when the horse is crooked or straight, when he is in a good position to the inside with his shoulders in advance of his hindquarters while remaining in front of the inside leg, or when there is too much bend in the neck. The ability to feel these positions will develop with experience. Having somebody on the ground to tell the rider what is happening or, better still, watching the movement regularly on video, will help too.

Counter-canter

The ability to hold the horse straight after riding half-pass will enable the rider to develop counter-canter in the correct way. The horse is bent round the inside leg of the rider in the

Left: A more advanced horse, clearly showing the moment of suspension in collected canter during the half-pass to the left.

Below: The same horse showing counter-canter left. Here the hind quarters are not so well engaged and there is a lack of collection.

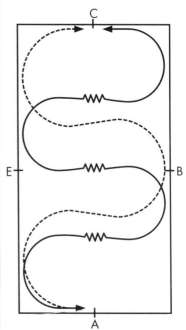

Left: The horse has been put in position left to turn on to a 10-m (33-ft) circle out of the corner. The rider will have to guard against the right shoulder falling out if the circle is continued in this position.

Above: A three- or four-loop serpentine. Used for making simple changes when crossing the centre line or for making loops in counter-canter.

half-pass and his body must then be straightened to the extent that there is a flexion to the inside and only a 'position' to the leading leg, rather than a bend similar to that in half-pass.

In counter-canter many riders tend to hold the horse with too much bend towards the leading leg. This causes the shoulders to fall away to the opposite side so that the hind steps do not follow the track of the front steps and the horse is crooked. In these circumstances, you must again maintain a very slight 'position' towards the leading leg and encourage the horse to remain straight by riding in this shoulder-in position without bending the neck.

At Medium level, the horse must perform counter-canter round the short end of the arena. This necessitates an advanced degree of control and balance which will not

Right: The horse turning on to a 10-m (33-ft) circle with the body following the line of the circle from head to tail. This position will enable the rider to keep good control of the shoulders.

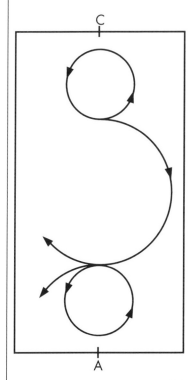

Above: An exercise in canter left with 10-m (33-ft) circles at each end of a counter-canter loop.

materialize if the rider maintains the counter-canter with too much bend in the neck. This minute degree of position to the leading leg keeps the horse straight and enables the inside hind leg to come underneath the body correctly to develop collection and keep the horse balanced.

At this stage of training, the horse will benefit from a lot of counter-canter. On a 20-m (66-ft) circle, transitions from trot to inside canter or outside canter (counter-canter) are excellent for developing control and obedience to the canter strike-off aids. Once the canter-trot transitions are good, graduate to simple changes on a circle, i.e. through walk. Make a three-loop serpentine between C and A, each loop going to the outside track, without change of leg. Alternatively, instead of following the end loops of the serpentine round to A or C,

151

make a 10-m (33-ft) circle as you cross the line from the counter-canter loop to increase collection and engage the inside hind leg before once more going back into counter-canter. A counter-canter figure of eight with a simple change at X often stops the horse from anticipating the simple changes. If the counter-canter becomes laboured or loses its jump, the canter must be freshened up by pushing the horse forward into a stronger canter to energise the hind legs and make sure the suspension has not lessened.

Developing extended and medium paces

The extensions have to be worked on and developed from the medium paces already established for Elementary level. In many cases, the younger, athletic horse will still be falling on his head when asked to take longer steps, while the older, stiffer horse, that has not been correctly trained from the start and whose career has covered other types of work, may have got into the habit of only lengthening the front steps and not coming through and covering more ground from behind.

It is important that the rein contact does not become stronger with the increased impulsion that must be created

Above: **Collected walk.**

Top right: **Extended walk.**

Bottom right: **Medium trot.**

152

Extended trot.

in a collected state. The horse is allowed to lengthen his out-line, most noticeably in the neck, together with the nose coming more in front of the vertical, and in the length of the steps, in order to cover more ground. In this extended outline, the front of the nose should be as far forward as the length of the step when it touches the ground. It is possible for the horse to take bigger steps within a short, compressed outline and therefore not lose his balance so easily, but this is not cor-rect, and in trot the front steps will often be flung up and out before drawing back to contact the ground if the head and neck are not allowed to lower and lengthen in the correct manner. If the hind legs give the impression that they are being left behind or are not actively stepping though under the body in trot or canter, this is a sure sign that the weight is predominantly on the shoulders.

154

Extended trot, showing a longer front step than hind step, with the neck a little short and the nose therefore not in line with the front foot.

In trot, it helps to work up to the bigger strides on a circle, having initially created impulsion with some shoulder-in and travers exercises. When the trot is sufficiently collected, ride the horse more forward in a stronger trot. The moment he feels heavier in the rein or loses rhythm, come back to collected trot. When the balance has been re-established, ride forward again. During this procedure, gradually increase the stronger trot until medium, and then some extended, steps have been achieved. It is difficult for any but very talented horses to make big extended steps on a circle, but preparing for extension in this way, by asking for lengthening on a circle, before asking for it on a diagonal or down the long side, makes it easier for the rider to regulate the horse's balance.

Riding some shoulder-in from the corner down the long side before moving across onto a diagonal or straightening out

155

A well-balanced and powerful medium trot.

into medium trot is beneficial for engaging the hindquarters, especially if the horse is inclined to fall onto one shoulder during lengthening. This will often happen on the stiff side. Before lengthening the stride, the shoulder-in will help to keep the horse even and balanced. Equally, if the same problem occurs, during the transition back to collection, a few steps of shoulder-in will help to lighten the shoulders and re-engage the hindquarters.

The importance of having an equal feel on both sides of the horse's mouth during the development of the extended trot cannot be overemphasized, as, if the horse learns to support himself on one rein or the other, there is a risk that the hind steps will become irregular, caused by the horse taking a long step with one hind leg and a short step with the other. Also, during the transition back to collection, the horse will not come back smoothly, staying on a straight line, but will set on the stronger rein and swing his quarters out to the side, therefore slowing down into collection on two tracks and making it obvious to the judges that he is not 'working through' but setting his jaw and his body against the aids. There is no value in making large and impressive extended steps over the diagonal line if the transition back to collection is not equally as good and therefore, at this stage, the horse must be trained to come back in a faultless manner as, in all dressage competitions from now on, the judges will put great emphasis on this ability.

In order to achieve good transitions from extension back to collection in both trot and canter, it is necessary to work really hard on the easier transitions where the horse has not so much impulsion to cope with. When trot to halt and canter to walk have been perfected, extension to collection will be easier. The most difficult transition for the Elementary and Medium horse to show in the arena is from a stronger canter back to a more collected canter, whether the differences are in extension, medium, working or collected. When training, time must be spent each day on a large circle in canter, alternating the speed without losing the rhythm and making sure that, when asked to open out in canter,'the horse does actually cover more ground and does not just hurry the steps.

Initially, the impulsion needed to cover the ground with bigger strides makes the horse come higher in the croup but, gradually, as the collection improves, the shoulders will not sink down as the steps lengthen and he will learn to stride out in a more balanced way, lowering the croup as he does so. In some Elementary and Medium standard tests, an extended canter is asked for from counter-canter. This is an extremely useful exercise to work on at home, as the counter-canter engages the hindquarters and when the horse is ridden forward from counter-canter the hind steps come through and lengthen out more readily.

The horse must also learn to build up impulsion in trot and canter, contain it and let it die down again without altering his speed. The ability to do this is usually only perfected at a more advanced level but the beginnings of this sort of control should be started at Medium level in as much as, prior to the point where the horse has to extend, some added impulsion must be put into the collected trot without altering the speed or rhythm so that, when reaching the diagonal, the contained impulsion can be released to make the longer, more forward steps.

More impulsion is needed for extension than for collection, which is why it is necessary to be able to store up a little for a short while before releasing it. The impulsion that is created by the more forward, freer steps in canter creates a problem when it comes to returning to a slower speed with shorter steps. The young horse cannot handle this impulsion, does not know how to ease off the power and is difficult to bring back to a working or collected pace. The old, stiff horse will set his jaw and back against the aids, which makes it difficult for him to come back easily or correctly. It is important, therefore, that the horse is kept obedient to the slowing-down aids and is properly taught how to manage his huge body when it is full of impulsion and how to apply the brakes correctly.

The movement of coming back to collected trot from an extended or medium canter is another test of being able to manage impulsion. When the transition is at the end of a diagonal, care has to be taken to keep the weight of the rider to the inside and to keep the direction of the horse to the leading leg until straightening up as the horse makes the first step of trot, otherwise the horse is likely to make a flying change when he loses balance. It is safer to come back to working canter for a few strides before asking for the trot, but it is not in order to slow down too far before the marker, as that is not what is asked for in the test and it will be marked down accordingly.

More advanced transitions, including rein-back

As the canter becomes more collected so the transitions into and out of canter become more fluent and should no longer be progressive. The simple change should now be canter to walk, two or three steps of walk and directly into the new canter lead. It is as well to introduce the horse to canter-halt transitions as they are required in all tests above Medium level and also in the three-day eventing tests that are sometimes used for Medium horses. Initially, in this movement, the horse will find it easier to make one or two walk steps before halting, but this must not become a habit as it will not be tolerated by judges in the more advanced tests.

The departure from rein-back is now sometimes required to be directly into canter. The legs are placed slightly back behind the girth to indicate to the horse to step back but, after the required amount of steps have been made, the legs must return to the 'on the girth' position before giving the canter strike-off aid for the leg that is required. A slight position to the leading leg must be maintained, so that the outside shoulder does not bulge away from the line. It is important that a straight rein-back is executed, in order to be able to make a straight strike-off into canter; a walk step is not allowed before the canter stride nor before the trot if the movement asked for is rein-back into trot.

Rein-back is a movement in which the horse automatically bends the joints in his hindquarters and therefore lowers his croup. As this is exactly what we are endeavouring to make the horse do in the collected gaits, rein-back can be used with discretion to encourage the horse to put more weight on the haunches, especially on occasions when he is a little onward-bound or on the forehand. A transition into halt, followed by one, two or three steps back (always vary the number of steps backwards), can do wonders for the balance.

It is a bad policy to use rein-back as a punishment because if the horse requires punishing, he will, in all probability, be very tense. If the horse is pulled back when he is tense, he will be made very uncomfortable and so will resent the movement in the future. The steps will be spoilt in as much as the feet will drag back and not be lifted above the surface of the arena. It is also possible that the steps will lose their diagonal sequence, to the extent that they appear lateral.

Competing at Medium level

When riding and competing at Medium level, much greater emphasis is put on the way the corners, turns and circles are structured. A horse that is collected, and who can execute a good shoulder-in, is able to be ridden through the corners of the arena as if on a quarter of a volte (6-m/20-ft circle). Likewise, when turning down the centre line, the rider can make an equally short turn at A or C, having ridden well into the previous corner instead of rounding off the two together as with a Novice horse. It is essential that the horse respects the outside leg when making these turns and does not deviate his quarters to the outside, thus riding the corners on two tracks. The rider must help the horse by keeping their weight well down into the inside stirrup, making sure their outside leg is in the correct position to stop the quarters moving out and also by using the inside leg on the girth to give the horse a support to bend round and so follow the more difficult line of the turn.

The same principles must be used when moving into

A medium horse showing a well-balanced working trot.

shoulder-in. The movement must not start as quarters-out. This is always more difficult on the centre line as there are no boards to discourage the quarters from deviating. The judge at C wants to see the hind legs remaining on the centre line as the shoulders are moved to the inside, with a definite line of three tacks and a bend through the whole body round the rider's inside leg. When preparing for, and riding into, shoulder-in at the desired marker, it is a help to establish the correct position of the neck first and then move the body into the bend.

A helpful exercise for controlling the quarters on the centre line is to ride about 12 m (40-ft) of travers to the right, then the same amount to the left, and so on, keeping the forehand exactly on the line, after which make some shoulder-in from the travers position, keeping the outside leg well placed as in the travers. This will indicate whether the horse performs good shoulder-in round the inside leg while the outside leg controls the quarters or whether, as so often happens, he escapes into a leg-yielding position by moving the quarters to the outside when being asked for shoulder-in.

If, during the test, the judge sees the quarters moving out instead of the shoulder being positioned in, he is justified in lowering the mark accordingly as the movement asked for will not have been shown in the desired way even if, later on down the line, the horse does appear to be in the shoulder-in position.

Similarly, the quarters must not escape to the outside on the 10-m (33-ft) circle in trot. A lack of impulsion will be more evident on a circle of this size, causing unlevel steps, while the hindquarters will deviate to the outside if the horse is stiff and not bending round the rider's inside leg, if the horse is not working through the rein or if the rider's weight slips to the outside due to a faulty position. When these problems occur on the circle, the movement directly afterwards will also be affected, i.e. the horse will not be straight on the

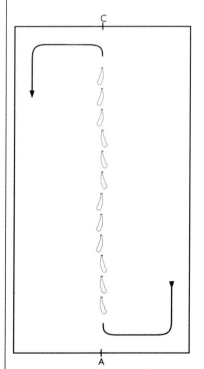

Travers to the right and left down the centre line.

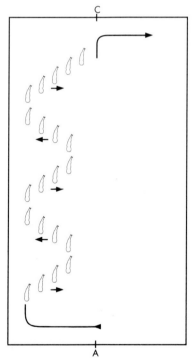

Half-pass into leg-yielding, repeated several times.

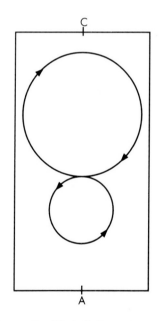

A 20-m (66-ft) circle in canter followed by a 10-m (33-ft) circle in trot in sequence, with a transition on the centre line. This exercise helps to keep the neck straight on the line of the circle because the new outside rein corrects any undesirable bend as soon as it occurs.

centre line or along the track, nor be able to move fluently into shoulder-in or half-pass.

When circling in canter, the quarters are most likely to deviate to the outside through stiffness and lack of collection, with the horse avoiding putting weight on the inside hind leg. The use of the rider's outside leg will correct part of the problem but thought must be given to why the quarters move to the outside in canter in order that better training may cure the cause. Too much bend in the neck on a circle will allow the shoulder to fall out and the quarters to deviate to the inside. 10-m (33-ft) circles, in both trot and canter, are a very revealing exercise for checking the suppleness, collection and flexibility of the horse and the correct position of, and application of the aids by, the rider. If the quarters deviate off the line of a 10-m (33-ft) circle in either gait, it is a sign that one of these is not sufficient.

Introducing and fitting a double bridle

At some time during a Medium horse's career, the double bridle should be introduced as, when he reaches Advanced level, it will become compulsory to use one. However, a double bridle should not be used if the contact in the snaffle bit shows any signs of unsteadiness during Medium-level work. It is a mistake to think that the purpose of a double bridle is to make the horse easier to control and bad horsemanship to use a curb bit to force the horse into a so-called 'better outline'. The double bridle should enhance an already consistent and acceptable connection, with the horse working through well to the rider's hand.

Great care must be taken when first fitting the snaffle and curb bits. Some horses with small mouths have very little room for two bits and it is difficult to make them feel comfortable. If the horse is used to an eggbutt snaffle bit, then it is wise to use a bridoon of the same design. Likewise, if a loose-ring or double-jointed snaffle has been used, a similar bridoon should be the first choice. The narrower the mouthpiece the more severe it is. However, very few horses have room in their mouth for a big, thick curb bit as well as a bridoon. Great attention should be paid to the size of the tongue when choosing the shape of a curb bit. A large, fleshy tongue, that lies on top of the lower jaw, will be subjected to a lot of pressure from a flat curb or one with a very small port. There are many curbs with various shaped ports and of different thicknesses in the mouthpiece. As they are all

A double bridle fitted correctly.

extremely expensive, it is advisable to borrow and try out one or two varieties before purchasing one and then finding that it is not the right design for your horse's mouth.

For the first double bridle, the cheeks should be short for a very sensitive Thoroughbred-type jaw and, in any other case, of only medium length until the horse has become used to the action of the curb. The long-cheeked curb has a greater leverage, especially if the upper cheek (the part above the mouthpiece) is short. A longer upper cheek lessens the severity, but I find that the curb chain will not fit snugly in the curb groove if the hooks for it are set too high on the bit. The curb chain should be covered with a rubber or leather guard to start with until the horse is familiar with the feeling, and it should be fitted so that a contact on the curb rein brings the

163

angle of the cheeks to 45 degrees to the horse's mouth. Personally, I prefer to use a covered chain at all times.

The first time a double bridle is put on, the plan should be to find suitable bits, fit them correctly but not to work the horse in them. The bridoon should be fitted with a slight wrinkle in the corners of the mouth as with an ordinary snaffle bridle. It should be exactly the correct width as if it is too wide it will interfere with the curb chain lying comfortably, as well as having a severe nutcracker action on the corners of the mouth. The curb bit should lie just below the bridoon. If it is too low, it may touch the tushes in a gelding's mouth and will, in any case, be more severe at the lower setting. Having selected and fitted what appears to be the right design for the horse's jaw and tongue, the cavesson noseband should be fastened at a height at which the skin will not be pinched between the noseband and the snaffle bit when a contact is taken up on the rein.

It is now advisable to familiarize the horse with the feel of the curb action by gently taking a contact in one hand with the snaffle reins and then, with the other hand, taking up the curb rein only to the extent that the horse becomes aware of the pressure of the curb chain on his chin. It is to be hoped that he will relax his jaw and give to this pressure, in which case he should be patted and the rein loosened. If there is a violent objection, the mouth is opened, the tongue drawn back and he tries to spit out the bit, it is obviously very uncomfortable and a different design should be tried. Personally, I do not think a horse should be worked in a double bridle until he is happy about accepting a contact on the curb rein while standing in the stable.

When he is being mounted, the snaffle rein only should be held, with the curb rein left lying on the neck or the buckle merely hooked over one finger. If the pressure of the curb chain is felt for the very first time while the horse is being mounted and he reacts in a violent way, a nasty accident could be the result.

The first few times the horse is worked in the school in a double bridle, the snaffle rein should be taken up, as with an ordinary snaffle bridle, and the curb rein should be slackened so that the horse merely feels the presence of the bit and the chain without experiencing any action from it. He should be ridden well forward and worked in a way that loosens him up, making sure that he does not object to the normal control of transitions nor of bending. When the rider is sure that the bits are not inhibiting the forward movement, a little more contact with the curb can be sought but the curb rein should never be stronger than the snaffle. The young horse will often dislike being bent, either to one side or both sides, when he feels the connection on the curb. The rider should be sensitive to this and make sure that the outside hand allows for the bend that is being asked for and does not restrict it in any way.

Holding double-bridle reins

There are several ways of holding the double bridle reins:

1 The snaffle rein goes round the little finger and the curb rein passes between the little finger and the third finger. Alternatively, the curb rein goes round the little finger and the snaffle rein passes between the little finger and the third finger. In both of these positions, the two reins come over the forefinger and are held in place by the thumb, just as when holding a single rein.

2 Another method is to have the snaffle rein round the little finger and over the forefinger, as with the single rein, and the curb rein passing between the little finger and third finger and out between the second finger and forefinger. This segregates the two reins totally and makes it very easy to shorten the snaffle rein only if they both get too long and too much curb is being used.

3 The snaffle rein passes over the top of the first finger and is held by the thumb with the curb rein loosely held under the fourth finger or between the third and fourth fingers and passing out between the first and second fingers. This method is a good one if it becomes necessary to ride the horse only on the snaffle because there has been a problem with the curb, as it is easy to keep a connection with the snaffle only and the curb rein can be kept longer and dormant until required.

4 The last method is called 'three in one'. It is used in the Spanish Riding School and is known as the classical way of holding the reins. The left snaffle passes round the fourth finger, the left curb goes between the fourth and third fingers, and the right curb is also in the left hand, between the second and third fingers. All three reins come up under the thumb as normal. The right snaffle rein is held in the right hand between the third and fourth fingers, as is normal for a single snaffle rein.

I believe it is necessary to have some form of anti-slip device on the snaffle reins as it is so important that they are kept at the correct length and do not creep longer so that they

The snaffle or bridoon rein is held between the third and fourth fingers. The curb rein passes between the second and third fingers, with both reins coming over the index finger and held under the thumb.

The bridoon rein passing below the fourth finger and the curb rein passing between the fourth and third finger. Both reins come out over the index finger.

The bridoon rein passing below the fourth finger and out over the index finger. The curb rein passing between the fourth and third fingers and out between the index and second fingers. This completely seperates the curb rein, making it easy to shorten the snaffle rein only when working.

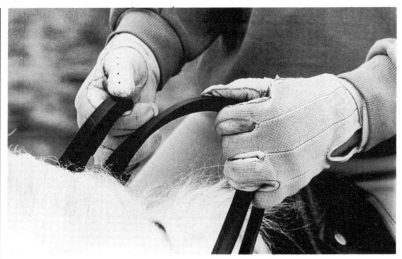

The bridoon rein is held above the curb rein and separated from it by the fourth finger, as shown here, or by the third finger as an alternative.

The bridoon rein passes over the index finger the other way round to the previous illustration and the curb rein goes round the fourth finger in the normal way. This is a suitable method of holding the reins if the snaffle rein only is used.

The three-in-one position as used in the Spanish Riding School. Three reins are held in the left hand and one rein in the right hand. The left bridoon passes round the fourth finger and the two curb reins are separated by the third finger with the right curb uppermost in the left hand. All three reins come over the index finger or the curb reins can pass below the index finger, as illustrated. The left hand should be held centrally over the withers. The right bridoon rein is held between the third and fourth finger in the right hand.

mistakenly become the same length as the curb rein and too much of the latter is put into use in error. A thin rubber rein, rubber only on the inside or leather stops on the rein are the most usual devices. Leather stops have the advantage that you can check that the reins are equal in length.

Gradually work the horse up to his normal way of going in the double bridle, introducing lateral work as he becomes used to the different feel. If he shows any sign of drawing back from the rein, he must be ridden purposefully forward using only the snaffle rein until he is taking the hand normally again. It is not necessary to have anything but an extremely light curb rein for the first sessions of wearing a double bridle. By 'session', I mean that you should work the horse for a few days until he is going as well as you could possibly expect and then go back to the snaffle bridle only for a short spell before using the double bridle again. I do not think it is of any value to ride the horse in a double bridle for one day only. It usually takes a few days for the horse to get used to the different feel and giving him several days to acclimatize to this is of more value. Likewise, just before a competition, always ride the horse in the double bridle for several days, to avoid any upsets. Obviously, these suggestions do not apply to an old, experienced horse that the rider knows well. With such horses, it can be better to ride in a snaffle while preparing for the test and then put on the double bridle just before it is time to compete, when the horse has loosened-up.

Riding-in for a competition

When riding-in for a test, it is a mistake to practise the exercise to any great degree. The first ten minutes, or longer if necessary, should be spent walking the horse round on a loose rein, letting him get used to the atmosphere and the lie of the land, etc. The next twenty minutes should be used to loosen up and relax the horse in trot and canter. After that is the right time to establish collection and ride a few exercises. If the horse's movements are not actually good enough for the current competition, no amount of work will improve them just before entering the arena. What really matters at this point is rhythm, relaxation and making sure the horse is in front of your leg and will move forward into extensions and come back to collection. Never have a disagreement with the horse when riding-in for a competition. The competition environment is often quite stressful enough, so a major priority should be keeping the horse really calm and letting him enjoy the situation and perform at his best. Never change your way of riding at a competition where everything should be as normal as in daily training at home. There is a tendency for riders who work alone at home suddenly to see other trainers and well-known riders doing something different, riding an exercise in what appears to be a superior way, etc. They are then tempted to influence their own horse in a similar manner but this is a grave mistake. To avoid tension and stress, the horse must remain confident and relaxed so that everything feels just the same to him at the competition as it always has done at home.

Each horse varies in the amount of time it takes to achieve the necessary relaxation at a new venue. Relaxation is evident when the horse is accepting the hand and the forward aids and will stretch down when allowed. Having relaxed him, the rider must then make sure the horse is supple, by using bending exercises, decreasing and increasing circles from the leg, etc. and asking for many transitions in all gaits. Only ask the horse to walk 'on the bit' when a sufficient degree of suppleness has been achieved, otherwise this is just the sort of situation where the walk steps can deteriorate due to anxiety and stiffness.

Only towards the end of the riding-in period should the horse be collected, remembering that the basis for collection is relaxation, suppleness, flexibility and obedience. The weight should now be transferred to the hindquarters, with increased elastic and energetic use of the joints, and relaxed self-carriage must be maintained. It is worth remembering the duration of work in collection that the horse is used to doing on a daily basis before having a break. It is no use working hard for ten minutes at home and then letting the horse have a rest if, at a competition, he will be worked for fifteen minutes without a break and then has to perform a ten-minute test in top gear. If the horse is not used to this routine, the energy required for this length of time may just not be available. When preparing for a competition test, never ride ultimate collection without proper suppleness.

After a pause to take the boots or bandages off, put your coat on, tidy up and apply fly spray if necessary, it is important that the horse should not feel that the day's work is finished and start preserving himself. Leave enough time after the stop to get back into gear with extensions in trot and canter and a few exercises from the test, thinking all the time of the rhythm and balance along with impulsion. When the time comes to ride round the arena, try to work round in both directions especially if there are flowers, judges' boxes or tables as opposed to cars. It is amazing how horses will discover different things to spook at from different directions. If the horse uses spooking as a way to hollow, disobey the leg or not think forward, make him work forward quite strongly in a slight shoulder-in position to keep him straight and on the aids. Some horse feel insecure when suddenly taken away from the working-in area and other horses. This is more likely to happen when the competition is large and the arena is roped off and surrounded by stands or cars, etc. It is important for the rider to stay very calm and relaxed at this stage so that any tension on the horse's part is not aggravated by the rider's own nerves. Think only of riding an accurate test; feel how the horse is going and make any improvements if possible.

The Advanced 60 x 20-m (198 x 66-ft) arena is much easier to ride in than the Novice arena of 40 x 20-m (130 x 66-ft). The corners do not come up nearly as quickly and therefore it is possible to keep the horse balanced with more impulsion. However, there are longer distances of straight lines for the judge to assess whether the horse is properly in front of the rider's leg or crooked due to insufficient control of the shoulders. The long centre line can be a problem if the horse is not regularly schooled on it. Neglecting work up and down the centre line will result in unnecessary low marks in a test, due to lack of control, which will be very obvious to the judge sitting at C. Work on this line should include perfect turns onto the line from both directions and halts from walk, trot and canter. Walk pirouettes made at either end of the centre line have a very calming influence, as you can stay on the line for as long as it takes to sort out a problem, as well as assessing the bend, the control of the shoulders and the effectiveness of the leg in the walk pirouettes. It is useful to have a video film taken of work on the centre line so that problems can be studied in detail later. Alternatively, somebody knowledgeable standing at the end to confirm what you are feeling is always a great help.

It is important to ride through the test at some time before the competition, especially if it is not possible to work in a large arena regularly. When the horse is first graded Medium, the unaccustomed size of the arena can be quite distracting until both the horse and rider become familiar with the new dimensions. The problem will not occur if the horse is always worked in a large manège. Similarly, if the young horse is always worked in a big space, a 40 x 20-m (130 x 66-ft) arena must be marked out so that suitable adjustments can be made.

It is often difficult for a big, long-striding hose to maintain enough impulsion in a small arena and it is advisable not to over-compete, especially on unsatisfactory surfaces, if the horse's paces are affected under these circumstances. The horse must associate going into an arena with working at his best, not with slacking off because the conditions are uncomfortable. Many riders will not compete in the small arena for these reasons, preferring to train their horses to Medium level before competing very much and only entering at the lower levels when the relevant tests are held in a 60 x 20-m (198 x 66-ft) arena.

It is sometimes of benefit to continue working the horse after completing the test, especially if he has not been as obedient as one would have liked. Horses are creatures of habit and if the rider always dismounts after completing a test, some of them can begin to think that the end of the work session is near at hand and 'switch off' during the last, vital ten minutes when they are required to perform at their best.

The competitions are only a test along the road to Grand Prix, to find out how your horse is progressing, to assess his character under competition situations and to establish if the judge is seeing what you are feeling. It must be remembered that the judges do not know what you are expecting in the test from your horse. They can only judge what they see and equate it with the standard of the day. A situation can often occur, therefore, whereby the rider can be pleased with the horse because some movement has been accomplished that has been a problem in training, but the marks are disappointingly low. Similarly, a horse can win a test when the rider has not had a good feel throughout but has managed to disguise the problems. A good competition rider will disguise problems, but this must not become a habit when training at home, where the horse must be schooled in a way that corrects all difficulties as they occur.

On riding the horse the day after a competition, it is most revealing to feel if anything has changed due to the stressful circumstances. Often, the horse will have reverted to problems that you thought you had cured long ago, such as being uneven in the rein, having too much weight on one or other shoulder or being difficult to straighten in canter on the centre line. These particular problems of each individual horse will always reappear from time to time and when they do it is wise to forget the test movements for a while and concentrate on re-establishing rhythm in the gaits, balance and straightness. The tests should be thought of as transitions in and out of walk, trot and canter with a few movements thrown in along the way. If the quality of the basic paces is kept correct to the level that is required, the movements will not be a problem.

The object of dressage is to enhance these basic paces and to improve the horse's physical stature and athleticism so that he is able to carry out the desired exercises in perfect harmony and co-operation with his rider.

If you wish to obtain perfection at Grand Prix level, however long it takes, the aspects of training up to Medium level, must be adequately established before any more difficult exercises are taught to the horse. It is easy to teach the horse the movements as though he is being trained for the circus but if the quality of the gaits and the harmony of the partnership are inhibited along the way, the end result will be a horse that is neither a pleasure to ride nor a joy to behold.

INDEX

Page numbers in *italic* refer to the illustrations